I Give Up

ALSO BY LAURA STORY

When God Doesn't Fix It: Lessons You Never
Wanted to Learn, Truths You Can't Live Without

What If Your Blessings Come Through Raindrops?

I Give Up

THE SECRET JOY OF A
SURRENDERED LIFE

LAURA STORY

with Leigh McLeroy

W PUBLISHING GROUP

AN IMPRINT OF THOMAS NELSON

Published in Nashville, Tennessee, by W Publishing, an imprint of Thomas Nelson.

Thomas Nelson titles may be purchased in bulk for educational, business, fund-raising, or sales promotional use. For information, please e-mail SpecialMarkets@ThomasNelson.com.

Any Internet addresses, phone numbers, or company or product information printed in this book are offered as a resource and are not intended in any way to be or to imply an endorsement by Thomas Nelson, nor does Thomas Nelson vouch for the existence, content, or services of these sites, phone numbers, companies, or products beyond the life of this book.

Scripture quotations marked csb are from the Christian Standard Bible. Copyright © 2017 by Holman Bible Publishers. Used by permission. Christian Standard Bible® and CSB® are federally registered trademarks of Holman Bible Publishers.

Scripture quotations marked esv are from the esv® Bible (The Holy Bible, English Standard Version®). Copyright © 2001 by Crossway, a publishing ministry of Good News Publishers. Used by permission. All rights reserved.

Scripture quotations marked THE MESSAGE are from *The Message*. Copyright © by Eugene H. Peterson 1993, 1994, 1995, 1996, 2000, 2001, 2002. Used by permission of NavPress. All rights reserved. Represented by Tyndale House Publishers, Inc.

Scripture quotations marked rsv are from the Revised Standard Version of the Bible. Copyright © 1946, 1952, and 1971 National Council of the Churches of Christ in the United States of America. Used by permission. All rights reserved.

Scripture quotations marked nasb are from the New American Standard Bible®. Copyright © 1960, 1962, 1963, 1968, 1971, 1972, 1973, 1975, 1977, 1995 by The Lockman Foundation. Used by permission. (www.Lockman.org)

Scripture quotations marked niv are from the Holy Bible, New International Version®, niv®. Copyright © 1973, 1978, 1984, 2011 by Biblica, Inc.® Used by permission of Zondervan. All rights reserved worldwide. www.Zondervan.com. The "niv" and "New International Version" are trademarks registered in the United States Patent and Trademark Office by Biblica, Inc.®

Scripture quotations marked nlt are from the Holy Bible, New Living Translation. Copyright © 1996, 2004, 2007, 2013, 2015 by Tyndale House Foundation. Used by permission of Tyndale House Publishers, Inc., Carol Stream, Illinois 60188. All rights reserved.

ISBN 978-0-7852-2630-7 (eBook)
ISBN 978-0-7852-2629-1 (TP)

Library of Congress Cataloging-in-Publication Data

Names: Story, Laura, 1978- author.
Title: I give up : the secret joy of a surrendered life / Laura Story, with Leigh McLeroy.
Description: Nashville : W. Publishing Group, 2019. |
Identifiers: LCCN 2019009001 (print) | LCCN 2019017313 (ebook) | ISBN 9780785226307 (E-book) | ISBN 9780785226291 (softcover)
Subjects: LCSH: Submissiveness--Religious aspects--Christianity.
Classification: LCC BV4647.A25 (ebook) | LCC BV4647.A25 S76 2019 (print) | DDC 248.4--dc23
LC record available at https://lccn.loc.gov/2019009001

Printed in the United States of America

19 20 21 22 23 LSC 10 9 8 7 6 5 4 3 2 1

I Give Up

I belong, I belong
To the maker of earth and seas
Who's as rich as a King
Yet so gentle and kind towards me

I am not cared for by a servant hired
But a Shepherd who would leave the ninety-nine

So when I give up, I gain
When I let go of having my own way
When I learn to see my surrender as a brand-new start
To know the fullness of my Father's heart

I will rest, I will rest
Not in worldly security
Not in what I may try to control that's controlling me
What if faith is simpler than I've made it be
Just a simple trusting in your love for me

So here's my life to take,
Though you've heard this prayer a thousand other days
Make this moment more than just empty words I say
Let it be a start
To know the fullness of my Father's heart[1]

Contents

Contents

PART ONE

Surrender...Who Me?

ONE

A Life Beyond Control

A dozen or so years ago, when Martin and I were newly-weds, we survived what we imagined to be the biggest trial we'd ever face. Martin was diagnosed with a brain tumor.

We had just moved to Atlanta from South Carolina and had only been married a short time. I was beginning a job with Perimeter Church as a worship leader, and Martin was enrolled in a great master's program in design.

Looking back, I realize we believed our time in Atlanta would be short. Once Martin graduated with his master's degree, we'd move back to South Carolina to be close to our families, then start a family of our own. Even if we didn't say so or put it down on paper, we had an X-marks-the-spot plan for our lives and believed God would get us there in the not too distant future.

For a while things seemed to be going very well. We

were adjusting to our new city and our new roles, making new friends and learning new skills. Then Martin began to have trouble staying awake. He even fell asleep once while he was driving, and again on a ski lift! His studies became too much for him to keep up with. My husband is smart—a far better student than I *ever* was. He was failing classes he normally would have aced. He could hardly stay awake to study and had little energy for even routine stuff. Other times his behavior just seemed odd. He'd ask me strange questions or forget really ordinary things, like whether or not we'd just unloaded the dishwasher.

We sought—and got—plenty of well-meaning advice: *Your husband needs counseling. He's just distracted—or lazy. Have you considered that it might be depression or some other form of mental illness?* We'd considered a lot of things. But we had zero answers. When we did meet together with a counselor, he told us that he didn't believe Martin's problem was related to any sort of mental illness. He thought it might be something physical instead.

So we made an appointment with a kind general practitioner recommended by a friend. She examined Martin and ran a battery of tests, but those were inconclusive. She recommended more testing and mentioned something about Martin's thyroid or his pituitary gland. We agreed to the procedures—a CT scan and an MRI—to see if those might point to something definitive.

I was out of town attending a worship conference with my Perimeter coworkers when the results came. The news was not good. Hearing your husband has a brain tumor is devastating. Seeing him struggle to do ordinary things is terrifying. The diagnosis was not what we had hoped for, but at least we knew for certain what was wrong.

I was frightened; I won't lie. But I pretty quickly transitioned into get-it-done mode. *We'll get through this. Martin will have the surgery he needs to remove the tumor, and then we'll get on with our lives, just like before.*

Nothing could have prepared Martin and me for what was in store for us.

After a successful surgery to remove the tumor pressing on his pituitary, Martin was readmitted to the hospital with complications that led to a second, emergency operation. That one left him in critical condition, heavily sedated for days, and he emerged with some challenging disabilities that we still work around today. It left both of us uncertain about the future we'd imagined and trying like crazy to adjust to a new normal that didn't feel normal *at all*.

My talented, hard-working husband wasn't going to be a full-time graphic designer (the career he was preparing for when the tumor was first discovered). And I wasn't going to be a stay-at-home mom like so many women in my family had been—or even a mom and a part-time songwriter/musician. Our plans changed drastically, almost overnight. We surrendered our vision of what our lives would be like for a version that was often created day by day on the fly.

There was no road map for the journey we were on. No mentor couple who could assure us they'd faced the very same challenges and come through them stronger than before—or at least come through them. This was uncharted territory, and we both knew it.

Before Martin's ordeal we'd always assumed we'd have

kids and looked forward to the day when we would be parents. But suddenly we weren't so sure anymore. How could we have a family when there were times we, ourselves, needed help just to get through an ordinary day?

I know we're not the only ones who've struggled with the decision about whether to have children. But our non-traditional lifestyle and Martin's lingering disability had us seriously questioning whether we were equipped for parenthood. We went back and forth, we prayed, and we spent hours talking it through with our wisest friends and advisors.

When I finally did become pregnant with Josie, our oldest, it seemed like the decision was made for us. We were going to be a family of at least three—and, somehow, we'd figure out the parenting logistics as we went. (Turns out there are no bestselling how-to books for artist-moms with crazy schedules and dads with short-term memory challenges either.)

Thankfully, Josie was the sweetest, most easygoing and resilient baby ever. By the time she turned two, she'd traveled with me to forty-eight states. She could sleep on a tour bus like a champ and buzz through sound checks with me like they were playdates with a handful of grown-ups she'd never met. At home, Martin and I were getting more comfortable with our day-to-day roles as partners and as parents. It didn't always look Pinterest-worthy, but with the help of our community, most days it was working.

I'd almost begun to feel like we had things under control again . . . until we learned I was pregnant with twins! We had hoped Josie would not be an only child. But we might have been thinking two was our limit. At least until an ultrasound revealed we would soon be outnumbered, three babies to two adults. With the arrival of Ben and Griffin, our home quickly became decorated with LEGOs, board books, stray socks, and half-eaten snacks. (You know the look, right?)

As crazy as it sounds with all we had going on, I think maybe we were starting to feel "in charge" again—at least a little. I was still working on the church staff at Perimeter, traveling to concerts, and writing and recording with three kids in tow. I even started working part-time on a doctorate in worship. Martin was coaching baseball and was active in our community, and together—with help—we were holding down the fort at home.

The very real threats to life and health that were once so pronounced, so terrifying, seemed to recede in the rearview mirror a bit. I may have even taken a deep breath and felt a sense of relief that it was all getting easier, somehow. (Or at least I was getting used to it!)

The boys were about to turn three when we learned we would be parents again. Just shy of forty, I was pregnant with baby number four—when only a few short years ago we weren't sure we'd ever be parents at all! I'll be honest: there were lots of things I'd envisioned doing for my fortieth birthday (a trip to Paris, maybe?), but having a baby was not exactly on our radar. Because of my age (What—you mean forty *isn't* the new twenty?) this was considered a high-risk pregnancy, and I had all the recommended screenings the doctor ordered. Except for a lot of fatigue, it was a dream pregnancy, and every regularly scheduled ultrasound ended with an enthusiastic thumbs-up and a "see you next time."

Until one didn't.

⟶

My thirty-seven-week ultrasound changed everything.

As I lay on the table and watched the murky screen, the ultrasound tech moved the wand across my belly to get a clearer picture of the little boy we were expecting soon.

His face came into view. And something was different. I looked more closely.

"What's that shadow?" I asked. "Do you see that?"

The tech was calm, but she was 100 percent focused on the same thing I was seeing. With a few clicks she captured the image and quickly called in the doctor.

Within minutes, I learned that our little boy would be born with cleft lip and cleft palate. The shadow we saw on his face told the story. In the last trimester of my third pregnancy with our fourth child, everything I knew about birth and caring for a newborn was being challenged. Any skill at mothering I'd managed to achieve up to that point did not include caring for a child with special needs.

I was stunned. I never saw it coming.

I drove to the appointment alone, but I was already thinking of how I would tell Martin and how we would tell our children. No part of me was thinking that I knew how to do this.

After the shock wore off, I felt a sadness begin to swallow up my dreams of the beautiful, flawless baby boy we expected, and I felt responsible too. *What could I have done to prevent this? What could I do now to lessen the impact of it?*

By God's grace, the ultrasound tech that day was the

same one I'd seen multiple times when I'd been pregnant with the twins. "Remember those perfectly healthy twin boys you had at thirty-eight weeks—the ones that didn't spend a day in the NICU?" she asked. "You didn't do or not do anything to cause that—and you didn't do or not do anything to make this happen either."

As the team dissipated, it was just the nurse practitioner and myself left in the room. I asked the most logical question, "So now what?"

"You grieve this," she answered simply.

Seriously? I was thinking of something tangible I could do—anything to help the situation. But my job wasn't to *do* anything. Instead, it was to surrender my expectations for the pregnancy and delivery we'd planned and for the perfectly healthy son we'd imagined bringing home. It was to give those up for something I could hardly even begin to wrap my brain around.

My one job now was to surrender. There was nothing else to do.

The homework I received that day was to readjust my expectations and relinquish my idea of a perfect baby—not yet knowing the extent of our son's challenges or how we would cope with what was ahead.

To make it even worse, I felt guilty for my heartbreak over the news. After all, other babies were stillborn, or had cancer, or had deformities that surgery couldn't fix. I would be handed a son with an imperfect face, yes. But he would be otherwise healthy, and the defect could be surgically repaired. Shouldn't I just get over it and deal? Even though it came like a bolt out of the blue, this wasn't the *worst* news

I could have gotten, right? And I'm a Christian. A pretty public one at that. Don't Christians trust God in every situation and give him glory no matter what?

They do. But they hurt too.

There was a lot we couldn't know for certain until our child was born. The doctors couldn't be sure of the extent of the baby's cleft lip and palate. We were told there might even be some involvement with his lungs and heart, as well. Or not. At the very least, we were looking at a more complicated delivery, feeding difficulties, and surgery for our baby at nine to ten weeks old—none of which were on my agenda until that day.

Martin's diagnosis, surgery, and resulting disability had required some serious surrender. An extended period of infertility did too. And when our three children arrived within three years' time, we surrendered any notion we might have had about getting along without the help of our extended community day to day. But this . . . this was a challenge of a different kind.

When I became pregnant with Josie, I waited a long time before decorating her nursery. I was thinking how devastating it would be if something went wrong. Now I *knew* something would be wrong, and I was powerless to change it. What needed to change most was *me*.

When I got home that day and told Martin, we shed some tears together. Then two things happened. First, we changed our son's name. I can't explain it, but my preferred name, Noah, just didn't seem right for him now. Martin had liked Timothy all along, and in that moment, we decided that his name was Timothy William (after our good friend and pastor, Bill). The other thing that happened was my husband stepped into the moment and became my comforter. I'm a strong person and don't often come unraveled, so the opportunities for him to do that day to day are kind of limited. But on that day, I was undone, and Martin stepped in to put his hand on me and tell me the truth we both needed to hear and believe: "It's going to be okay. No matter what."

Individually and together, we talked to our pastor friend Bill (who really should be on the payroll—he's helped us so much through the years!), and we both began to feel more hopeful and encouraged. I remembered Bill saying to me about another, earlier challenge, "I think in this season of life you need to wait on the Lord."

"Yes! That's it! I need to wait on God. Great! What steps do I take to do that?"

"You're not getting me, Laura," Bill had said. "Wait is wait. There are no steps. You just surrender. And then you sit tight."

This time, Bill simply loved us and said, "I don't know what to say. I hurt for you both." And that was enough, in the moment. But I also heard God say, *Give me this, Laura. And wait on me. I've got you.*

Ah, that surrender thing again. Hadn't I learned it yet?

I can't say that the weeks between the diagnosis and Timothy's arrival were easy. They weren't. While I made a conscious decision to trust God and surrender my expectations to him, I also did what anyone in similar circumstances would do: I searched the internet for information about cleft lip and palate and clicked through picture after picture of babies born with it. Let me tell you, friend, my heart sank. That little exercise did nothing to decrease my anxiety.

I don't recommend doing this or the other fruitless thing I did at first: imagining all the picture-perfect new baby photos of friends on social media or the "March babies" bulletin board in our church's nursery. It's just not helpful—at all—to meditate on what we fear or dread.

Instead, God tells us to consider him, to immerse ourselves in his Word, and to meditate on his truth.

I remembered a lesson from Psalm 1 I'd shared not too long ago with some new moms in our church, and now it really seemed perfect for me. It begins like this:

> Blessed is the one
>> who does not walk in step with the wicked
>>> or stand in the way that sinners take
>>>> or sit in the company of mockers,
>> but whose delight is in the law of the LORD,
>>> and who meditates on his law day and night.
> That person is like a tree planted by streams of water,
>> which yields its fruit in season
> and whose leaf does not wither—
>> whatever they do prospers. (Ps. 1:1–3 NIV)

It's not wrong, I had told them, to want to be favored, fortunate, blessed. But it *is* wrong to expect the world to deliver those things to us. Instead, our blessedness or happiness comes from considering what God says about himself and this world. Meditating on this makes us strong, like fruit-bearing trees planted by fresh streams.

When we're rooted in God and in his Word, we're positioning ourselves for a blessed life, regardless of our circumstances. And what is it, exactly, that rooted trees "do"? Nothing! They simply stay put, right where they are, their deep roots soaking in all that's needed for a good and fruitful life.

"You and I just need to remain rooted in God," I told them. "None of us is planted here by chance. No matter what, our assignment is to remain in him, to receive what we need from him, to be still and trust him. He's going to do the rest."

The biggest problem with being a teacher is that sometimes you have to swallow your own lessons whole, like I had to swallow that one. I absolutely believed it when I'd said it to them. No doubt about it. How could I believe it any less now, when it applied so specifically to me?

Before this last pregnancy, I'd started the practice of getting up very early each morning and sitting quietly on the sofa with my Bible and a cup of coffee, drinking in the words I knew I needed more than anything—even more than a few minutes of extra sleep.

Honestly, this practice probably began less out of deep, spiritual commitment than from a desperate desire not to do bodily harm to my children before the day was done! My record in keeping this appointment has not been perfect by any means. I miss plenty of mornings. But over time my kids have gotten used to seeing me there, alone and quiet. I figure if they ever ask, I'll just say, "Mommy needs time with Jesus or she will implode." Because Mommy does!

Now, waiting for Timothy's arrival, I needed that time more than ever. Because the challenges don't stop coming, even when you've done this life of faith thing for a long time. They bombard you, like C. S. Lewis said, "the very moment you wake up each morning. All your wishes and hopes for the day rush at you like wild animals. And the first job each morning consists simply in shoving them all back; in listening to that other voice, taking that other point of view, letting that other larger, stronger, quieter life come flowing in. And so on, all day."[1]

I need that "stronger, quieter life" like I need air. I tend to think of every hardship or challenge as a complication in my "normal," chilled-out state. But these things aren't complications, really. They're just *content*. They're normal life, actually. We live in a world broken by sin. Bad things happen. They even happen to "good" people, and they always will. But for those of us who follow Jesus, our challenges and heartbreaks are not the last word. The world doesn't offer that. Only Jesus does.

Every dark place on the landscape of our lives is a place where we can realistically hope to see God's goodness and glory break through. That's just how he rolls.

In the past, Martin and I have both had a tendency to see his disability as an inconvenience rather than as a tool in God's hand—a way for his glory to be displayed. But God has kept on doing good things we could never have planned or realized through this unique, unwanted circumstance.

We have more compassionate, empathetic children, I'm sure, than we might have otherwise had. We've had to slow down at times and take life at a less accelerated pace, and that has allowed us to see and enjoy things we might have otherwise missed. We've had to rely on others to help us through logistical challenges because Martin can't drive. But even that complicating circumstance has allowed us to build true friendships and invest more in the lives of others here in our Atlanta community. We're not waiting to go somewhere else now. We're home.

I'm not really much of a *why* person. I've discovered that knowing why a thing happens or doesn't happen doesn't change much. But since the Monday afternoon of that ultrasound and the hard news about our baby boy, I've become more focused than ever on *what* and *who*.

What do I know is true? I am extravagantly loved. And I am not in control. Not even a little. Who is in control? God is. He has my good in mind, and he is 100 percent ready to display his glory in and through my weakness. My only job is to trust him. To surrender.

෬

When Martin and I told our kids about baby Timothy's face, we were a little apprehensive about how they'd take the news. But we shouldn't have been. The boys are young, sure, but we anticipated at least a few questions.

"We need to tell you something about the new baby," we began. "His face is going to look different than other babies' faces. He's going to have a funny lip, and some people might think it looks strange or scary. You might even think so too."

They thought about this for a second. "Okay," they said. "Can we go play now?" And that, as they say, was that.

Josie understood a little more; she did have a question. "The crack in his lip, is it hurting him?"

I could have died with love for her when she asked that. Her care for her baby brother was that sweet.

"No," I said. "It doesn't hurt him. It may make it hard for him to eat, and he'll have to have an operation to fix it, but he won't be hurt." Then I went on, just to be sure she understood: "His face is going to look really different from other babies' faces. Some people may not understand or might look at him funny, but to us he'll look normal."

Then she looked me in the eye and said, "But we're gonna love him anyway because he's *family.*"

Oh, yes, baby girl. Yes, we are.

The Sunday before Timothy's scheduled arrival, our family stopped for lunch at a little Mexican restaurant—one we'd never been to before. We were one of three families there, but the place was so small it seemed full. A woman who'd been to Perimeter that same morning and heard our pastor's announcement that I was giving birth the next day—as if it wasn't already obvious I was about to pop!—walked up to me. She asked where I was having the baby, and when I told her, she said she'd just become the head nurse for their labor and delivery unit—I mean the head cheese over all of it. (You just can't make this stuff up. God knows everybody, right?)

She assured me she would be there the next day and walk me through anything I might need help with (short of having the baby, of course), and she totally did. That little "coincidence" was a well-timed and tender reminder that God was already out ahead of me, paving the way and meeting our family's needs. It's one thing to believe he has "angels" at their post, ready to work on our behalf. It's another thing altogether to meet one over a plate of enchiladas.

As great as I felt about that little reminder of God's love and provision, the next morning did not exactly go as planned. (Welcome to life in the Elvington household!)

Instead of waiting to go into labor, I'd scheduled an induction, mostly so that we'd have childcare nailed down for Josie, Ben, and Griffin. But when we arrived at the hospital at our appointed time of 1:00 p.m. and were admitted into a room, the room's monitoring system wasn't working properly and didn't get fixed until early evening. So the birth we'd planned for that day didn't actually happen until the next morning.

When I'd been asked to confirm my birth plan, I kept my wishes short, sweet, and very direct: "I'd like this baby out of me, and I'd like to not feel it *at all*." Well, at least one of those two things happened. The epidural I got apparently didn't work, and let's just say I got to feel an enormous amount of the beauty of childbirth.

Then one more thing happened that I didn't expect: when Timothy was born, I looked down at my precious nine-pound, eight-ounce son with his separated lip, and I saw a perfect, angelic face. I mean, I thought he was just about the sweetest thing I'd ever seen! Any anxiety I'd had about what I would think or feel when I laid eyes on him disappeared in an instant. Any worry over whether or not I would have trouble bonding with him vanished. In that moment I just saw . . . perfection.

Almost as soon as I held him for the first time he was whisked away, while Martin and my parents looked on. After a few seconds I heard my mom say, "Praise God!"

"His chart says cleft lip and cleft palate," said the nurse, "but there's no break in his palate." Everything beyond his lip was intact and as it should be. The complications were far less severe than what we'd been told to expect—a very sweet surprise, indeed.

Even with that great news, we were still on an enormous learning curve with Timothy. Feeding him was a challenge from day one; even though he might be sucking, there was no guarantee he was getting the milk he needed. The first few days of his life he lost weight (thank goodness for those healthy nine pounds and eight ounces he started with!) at a rate that seemed a little alarming, at least to his mom. But pretty quickly we met with a whole fantastic team of craniofacial experts who would become like family over the next few months. A surgeon, nurse, nutritionist, speech pathologist, and occupational therapist described what our son would experience over the next several weeks, and we simply tried to take it all in, moving forward a day at a time.

Through it all, we felt their support and the support of our church and community. Meals appeared miraculously at our door. Errands were run. The kids were bathed and fed, even when my hands were full. The boys quickly invented their own expression of solidarity with their new baby brother: Timothy had a small piece of surgical tape he had to wear over his lip, and for days Griffin and Ben found tape and pressed it over their own top lips too. (Good grief. What's not great about being three?)

18

Once again, our plans were upended for a different kind of "normal": the peaceful maternity leave I'd first imagined instead became a crazy hopscotch of doctors' appointments and daily challenges with Timothy's weight and feeding. But when my plans are blown to pieces, I begin to see *his* plans unfold, and he promises that they are good: "'For I know the plans I have for you,' declares the LORD, 'plans to prosper you and not to harm you, plans to give you hope and a future'" (Jer. 29:11 NIV).

Keep telling me, Lord. I'll get it eventually. I promise.

I understand that surrender may seem all but forced when the obstacles we face are super-sized. (No doubt our little family has experienced more than a few of those.) For instance, you'd have to be crazy to believe you're in charge of brain tumors or infertility or a baby born with an obvious birth defect. Most people would say those kinds of things—and plenty more—are simply beyond our control.

But what about when the challenges seem more, I don't know, ordinary? Is complete, open-handed surrender still the secret to a blessed life? Is it still the door that opens into God's presence, where the psalmist insisted there is "fullness of joy" and "pleasures forever" (Ps. 16:11 NASB)?

I believe it is.

Not just in the losses but even in the victories, surrender is the secret to a life of joy. Before I knew how true they were (and believe me, I'm still learning!), I wrote and sang these words:

The sweetest sound, the highest praise,
Is the letting go of this life You gave.
Our greatest prayer, an act of faith,
Is an open hand; Lord have Your way . . .
Jesus, I surrender all—every victory and loss
Take it all, take it all, 'till all I have is open hands.[2]

Being a woman who is absolutely in control of her own life is not a goal I need to aspire to. That kind of woman might look appealing on TV—but I don't believe that's possible. Not really. In my best moments, I want to surrender my life to the one who loves and cares for me. Who knows and does what is best and brings himself glory in the process. Because he deserves it.

And I'm thinking you might want that too.

WHITE FLAG PRAYER #1

God, I give up. I surrender now my need for control and ask you to begin a work in my life. Amen.

TWO

Dear God: Let's Be Co-Rulers. Love, Me

Americans seem to be especially enthralled with gorgeous historical dramas like *The Crown* and *Victoria*. Maybe you've watched one and loved seeing the elaborate palaces and incredible costumes. These shows portray young, beautiful women with absolute power. Even most heads of state bow to queens—no matter their age or experience. Guests are expected to leave their presence walking backward. A queen speaks, and important things happen. Prime ministers and heads of state jump to do her bidding. Her every need seems to be anticipated and met—by lots of attendants—and fast!

We're drawn to these shows and captivated by them, but

we know that lifestyle is not realistic for any of us. Yet don't we kind of expect something similar to that with God?

Here's what has to be one of the worst life plans ever hatched: "I know I don't get to be in charge, but maybe God and I could co-reign. If we did, I'm sure I could be a huge help to him."

I mean, why not do the two-rulers-for-the-price-of-one thing? I would never insist on ruling alone. Of course not! We could trade authority back and forth between us, depending on who's offering the better idea for my life at the time. (Naturally, I'm going to be the best judge of this.) One day God might be 100 percent in charge, but the next day it could just as easily be me. We could divide things fifty-fifty or assign categories: *You take health, God. I'll take finances.*

It sounds pretty ridiculous when you say it out loud or see it in print, but I'll bet you've considered this reigning-with-God arrangement more than once. I know I have. Here's the problem: crowns are made for one head, not two. Thrones are designed as single seats, not love seats or sectional sofas. The very word *sovereign* doesn't suggest a committee—just the opposite. So there can, by definition, be only one sovereign entity. Only one supreme authority. Only one being who wields absolute, unlimited, boundless and full authority and control. And that wouldn't be me.

It's one thing to momentarily resist God's authority or question his ways. Every one of us has done that at one time or another. But if I really believe co-reigning with God over my life is a viable life option, then I have seriously misunderstood him, not to mention overrated myself.

Do you remember the movie *Bruce Almighty*? Bruce Nolan, an obscure television reporter in Buffalo, New York, blows his stack after a particularly frustrating day at work. When he flies into a rage and gives God a piece of his mind, God gives *him* a temporary taste of what it's like to run things. Bruce suddenly has all of God's power but none of his wisdom, so he makes some pretty dumb and selfish choices with predictable consequences. It doesn't take long for Bruce to realize that being sovereign isn't nearly as easy or as fun as he imagined.

Bruce Almighty reminds me of something I've already learned from experience: men and women make awful gods! Unlike the one true God, we are weak, wisdom-limited, vision-challenged, petty, proud, and easily fooled. We underestimate our flaws and overestimate our strengths, even on our best days. That's why we need him, and that's why we need to surrender control to him. Not just a little bit, either. All of it, all the time.

If you come to my house, you will not see a throne room or a throne-like piece of furniture anywhere. But there *is* a throne in my heart. And there's one in yours too. There is a seat of power, influence, and control inside of me where decisions are made and habits are established. Where questions of right and wrong are weighed—and questions of better and best are too. It's a place where I entertain some thoughts and dismiss others. Where my perceptions about myself and the people around me are formed. And the question I have to answer not just once and for all but again and again every day is, Who is sitting on the throne of my heart?

"Who sits on the throne of your heart?" isn't the same question as "Are you a Christian?" or "Who do you say is Lord?" If you've trusted Jesus for the forgiveness of your sins, then those are pretty easy to answer. "Who sits on the throne of your heart?" is asking, "Whose voice do you believe and whose commands do you follow, day in and day out?"

For me, the biggest challenge to this question is almost always my own emotions. In other words, sometimes a gap exists (and not always a small one!) between how I feel and what God's Word says is true. When I base my decisions, words, actions, or beliefs on how I feel, I am on the throne. When I base my decisions, words, actions, or beliefs on what God says is true, then he is on the throne.

Please understand that I am not saying emotions are bad. They're not! In fact, they are good—the very essence of life. God made us feeling people by design and not by accident. He gave us our emotions, and they can really enrich our lives when they're owned, understood, and acted on in the right way.

The Bible is full of stories with plenty of powerful emotional punch—stories of hope and longing and sorrow and joy. Throughout its pages we see real people who experience the highs and lows of life in all its glory. And that's not all. In God's Word we also see Jesus displaying emotions. He was moved to tears by the death of his friend Lazarus. He felt compassion for the masses who had nothing to eat, so he fed them. He heard the cries of ten lepers who longed for healing, and in his love and pity, he made them whole.

He struggled in prayer on the night before his crucifixion and pleaded with his Father for the cup of suffering to be removed from him, if God would have it be so (John 11, John 6, Luke 17, and Matt. 26:39).

The fully divine *and* fully human Son of God has felt every feeling you and I can feel. But he was not ruled by any of those feelings. Instead of being ruled by his emotions, Jesus was ruled by the will of his Father. It shaped every step of his journey. He said to those who were following him, "For I have come down from heaven, not to do my own will but the will of him who sent me" (John 6:38 ESV).

That's the touchstone of truth he returns to over and over again.

When Jesus was tempted by Satan and felt tired, hungry, and threatened, he didn't let those very human emotions dictate his responses. Instead, he did exactly what you and I need to do: he relied on what God said was true—about life, about his situation, about his Father, and about himself.

Do you remember the story?

After his baptism, Jesus retreated alone to the wilderness for forty days and forty nights. Satan followed him there, waiting for the right time to tempt him. Three times, he suggested to Jesus things he might do to take care of his own needs . . . to make himself feel better . . . to rule his own life.

Knowing Jesus had fasted, Satan appealed to his feelings of hunger—and challenged his identity—in one single dare: "If you are the Son of God, command these stones to become loaves of bread" (Matt. 4:3 ESV). (Boy, that must have sounded good!) Jesus had more than enough power to do just that. But instead, he trusted what God said about his deepest hunger and about his role as the incarnate Son of God: "Man shall not live by bread alone, but by every word that comes from the mouth of God" (v. 4 ESV).

But Satan doesn't quit—not even when he's behind.

He tempted Jesus again, taking him to Jerusalem, to the highest point of the temple. "If you are the Son of God," he said again, "throw yourself down, for it is written, 'He will command his angels concerning you,' and 'On their hands they will bear you up, lest you strike your foot against a stone'" (v. 6 ESV).

Once more, Jesus resisted the temptation to do what he could have easily done, revealing his identity as God's Son and showing Satan a thing or two in the process!

"'Again it is written,' he said, 'You shall not put the Lord your God to the test'" (v. 7 ESV). (Are you seeing a pattern here?)

For a third time, Satan challenged him, showing him all the kingdoms of the world and their glory: "All these I will give you, if you will fall down and worship me" (v. 9 ESV). Hold on there. Was Jesus a king? He was. Did he deserve a kingdom and glory? He did. Was that promise Satan's to deliver? It was not.

"Then Jesus said to him, 'Be gone, Satan! For it is written, "You shall worship the Lord your God and him only shall you serve"'" (v. 10 ESV).

Jesus showed us what do when we are tempted to replace God's designs with our own desires. *We don't have to let our emotions reign.* We can rely instead on what God says is true.

Instead of distorting our God-created affections and

making mini-gods of them, we can stand on the rock-solid reality of God and his Word. Our emotions may change dozens of times in the course of a day. If you and I relied on them as the basis for our decisions and actions, think how unstable our lives would be!

What would happen if I let loneliness reign over all my decisions?

What would happen if I let fear determine my activity or inactivity?

What would happen if I let jealousy or unforgiveness dictate my responses in all my relationships?

My life would be complete anarchy, that's what! I would have no peace. No security. No hope. No joy. And that, my friend, is no way to live.

Co-reigning is futile and needless. We have a King. He is good and loving and wise. We should rely on him—and him only.

There's another good reason I should stay off the throne and leave the ruling of my life to God: I have a proven tendency to mess things up. I have good intentions and even a few really good ideas. But sometimes things can go sideways so fast that I find myself questioning not only my actions but also my worth as a child of God.

Not too long ago, I traveled to The Cove in Asheville, North Carolina, to lead a conference with my good friend Lisa Harper. The Cove is a fantastic retreat center run by the Billy Graham Evangelistic Association and a place I always look forward to visiting. To do the retreat with Lisa was an added blessing, and I looked forward to our time together.

My parents live just about an hour away from The Cove, so I went up a day early with Josie and the boys, glad to have the extended time for a visit. The morning after we arrived, I sat downstairs in Mom and Dad's den in my pajamas, enjoying a cup of coffee and some much-needed down time. Josie, Ben, and Griffin were already out of bed and playing, running up and down the stairs—but I suddenly realized I hadn't heard them in a while. About the time I got up to go and check on them, the doorbell rang. When I opened the door, I saw the boys in their pajamas, standing with the next-door neighbor's gardener, who explained that he'd found them alone outside and thought he'd better bring them home.

My sons were three, and they were playing unsupervised near a busy street. I didn't even know they'd left the house, but somehow, they'd gotten outside. They could have easily left the yard and run into the street or even wandered down to the creek that ran behind the house.

I thanked this guardian angel with a Weed eater and brought them back inside, but I was really shaken. I had let my sons out of my sight, and although they were back home and safe, in my mind's eye I saw every awful thing that might have happened to them but didn't. For the rest of the day I thanked God for their safety and the gardener's kindness, and I felt horrified that I had been relaxing on the sofa while their little lives might have been in danger.

That night I fell asleep at The Cove still feeling anxious and full of remorse. About 3:00 a.m., I woke up, and the

Devil was having a field day with my emotions! The accuser was accusing me, and I was buying every bit of what he was selling.

What made you think that you could take care of these boys? Why should you have been blessed with children? You don't even know when they're in danger!

I laid there and wept over what had happened and thought how a better, more "qualified" mother would have noticed sooner that her children were missing, would have already been out searching for them, calling their names. Heck—a better mother would have them gathered at her feet, telling them Bible stories or making crafts while a homemade breakfast simmered on the stove. I felt sick in my soul and completely unworthy—not just for motherhood but for anything at all, including the weekend ahead.

One of the songs I'd already selected to play for this retreat was "Good, Good Father" but the song on repeat in my head that night sounded more like "Bad, Bad Mother." I heard it loud and clear: "You're a bad, bad mother, that's who you are, that's who you are . . ." By the time morning came I was in Lisa's room, choking out the story and feeling like the biggest loser-parent on the planet.

"I'm a failure and phony," I told her through my tears. "I'm here trying to pretend I have it all together, but my kids could have drowned in a creek yesterday! I don't deserve them, and I don't deserve to be here!"

Lisa was wise enough to understand the very real spiritual warfare I was experiencing, and she prayed for me. That's what good friends do. When she was done, she reminded me that my children have a Father who will never, ever fail them and who sees them and looks after them even when I cannot. That was the truth I needed to hear.

I have no illusions about being perfect; most days I'd settle for just adequate. But being a mom has made me realize how much I need Jesus. How much I need grace. And how grateful I am that he *is* a good, good Father who loves me beyond reason—even on my worst days. Why would I ever imagine I'm as qualified as he is to rule my life?

One more thing about competing with God for control: it's hardly ever a one-and-done deal. We're never *completely* surrendered—at least not for long. I've heard it said that living sacrifices have a way of crawling right off the altar, and boy, do they ever. Even though I believe and agree that God deserves and should have 100 percent authority and control over my life, I sometimes take a little back.

It happens when, like my ancestor Eve, I imagine that God does not have my very best in mind. That he may be holding out on me, keeping things from me that are good—things that I "deserve." I let fear grab my heart and decide that, since my life feels chaotic, God has no plan for it. (And if he doesn't, then I'd better create one, and fast, right?) Or I feel ashamed of my sins and imagine that God has thought twice about forgiving me and instead is waiting to punish me. So I run from his presence—the *only* place where there is "fullness of joy" and "pleasures forever" (Ps. 16:11 NASB), resolving to do better next time—on my own. Or I let my circumstances dictate my understanding of God, instead of allowing him to help me understand my circumstances.

There are times, as we continue to hope for healing for Martin's illness, that I question whether God has dealt bountifully with us. I struggle to say with the psalmist that the lines have fallen for us in "pleasant places," that we have a "delightful inheritance" (Ps. 16:6 NIV). Some days don't seem so pleasant at all, and I don't want to agree that the lines have fallen anywhere; I want them to *move*. If he really is good and really does love us, won't God just heal my husband and make his disability go away?

On a good day, I can rely on God's Word and my past experience of his faithfulness to help me surrender my will to his. On a good day, I can say, "This is how I feel, God— but what you say in your Word is true." But let's face it: not every day is a good day.

So when the battle for control begins again—and it will—what do I do?

- I acknowledge the struggle. (Denying it doesn't help. I know. I've tried.)
- I confess my strong desire to be in charge, and I name my fear of not being in charge.
- I admit that my emotions do not always tell me the truth about my circumstances or about my God.
- I search God's Word for truth and keep it always before me. I read it. I pray it. I sing it. I write it on my hand with a ballpoint pen if I need to. I have it ready.
- I remind myself of God's faithfulness to his children throughout history and of his faithfulness to me.

Then I do the next thing I would do if I were surrendered to God on this day, in this situation, at this moment. Because the smallest act of trusting obedience can serve to remind me of the one who loves me, who sees me, who has my back, and who's already gone out ahead of me to make a way.

And finally, I relax.

Because I don't need more of me on the throne.

I need more of him.

WHITE FLAG PRAYER #2

God, I don't want to compete with you for control of my life. You know me—all my fears, impatience, and, at times, even my unbelief. Holy God, Creator of the universe, help me to daily surrender to you as the Lord of my life.

PART TWO

Who Do I Surrender To?

THREE

A Great, Good, Trustworthy God

Let's say you need an operation on your heart. You can't do it yourself, obviously. You're going to have to trust a professional to open you up and fix whatever is wrong. You probably have a few criteria for someone who will crack your chest and take your heart in their hands, right? At minimum, he or she is going to need many years of study, a current medical license, and maybe a little gray hair. It would also be reassuring if they were considered tops in their field. Better yet, maybe they've operated on someone you know, so you've seen the results of their expertise firsthand. Or perhaps they've developed and perfected the very procedure or technique they'll be using on you. (Extra points if it is named after them and written up in medical journals!)

Way before the moment the anesthesiologist comes in to put you to sleep, I'm guessing you will have surfed the internet and learned as much as you can about your surgeon: how many times they've done this operation, what kind of success they've had, where they studied, and how other patients have rated them. You will have met Dr. So-and-So at least once and asked whatever questions you have about this scary thing that is far, far beyond your ability to control.

While you are unconscious, that doctor will be working hard on your behalf. You won't contribute a thing, as you will have surrendered 100 percent control of your surgery to someone else. This is as surrendered as most of us will ever get, and as much research as we might have done, we will still be giving up control to a stranger.

As unnatural as it may feel, you and I are created to consciously surrender control of our lives—heart, mind, body, and spirit—to God. Not to a theory or a force or the cosmos. To the one God who is Father, Son, and Holy Spirit—who has created us, loves us, and set a plan in place to draw us to himself and care for us forever. He knows and wants to be known by us. This is made possible through the person of his Son, Jesus. It's not enough for us to just know about him. We aren't convinced to trust by what other people tell us about God or what we've read in books. We come to trust him when we know him by experience.

Anyone who's had a child knows that it's one thing to love your child before you meet him or her for the first time, but it's another thing altogether to hold that child in your arms. Until your baby is finally yours at birth or adoption, you love them, sure, but with a vague and hopeful kind of love, a love that is deeply and sincerely felt but pretty short on specifics.

Our entire family fell in love with Timothy from the moment we knew we were expecting another child. Once Martin and I got over the shocking idea that we'd be parents of a newborn again, we were smitten. Josie, Ben, and Griffin kissed, patted, and talked to the bump that was Timothy for months. In the same way, we've been crazy about each one of our kids from the first day we knew they existed. But staring at an ultrasound image is not the same as holding the perfect, squishy little person you've carried for nine months or dreamed of for longer.

Once your baby arrives, you're no longer dreaming. You come to love particular things about them—like the funny sound of their hiccups, the cute dimple in their chin, the warm weight of their sleepy body in your arms, and in Timothy's case, even the tiny split from his nose to his upper lip that only weeks before his birth had almost frightened us to death. We love *this boy* and his unique presence in our lives.

If you asked any one of us why we love him, we could tell you—talking for days, and in more detail than you might be willing to sit still for! Josie thought her new baby brother was so special that she asked me to bring him to her classroom show-and-tell when he was only a few weeks old—and I did. (Yes, these are the things you'll do with number four that you wouldn't have even considered with your first!) She wanted her classmates to know her baby brother, too, and I understood why.

Over time, I've come to know a very real God through

my experiences with him and through his Word. He's not just the God of Abraham, Isaac, and Jacob; he's my God too. He didn't just part the Red Sea for Israel when they faced sure death by Pharaoh's army; he's also made a way for me in more "impossible" situations than I can count.

I love the story of how he guided his people in the wilderness with a cloud by day and fire by night. And when I'm lost or confused or don't know which way to go, he guides me too. It matters that he's the God of history, for sure—but it matters just as much that *we* have history, him and me, and that I know his goodness and power and faithfulness, not just from my study of him but from my life with him.

I'm especially encouraged by the Psalms—the very personal journals of men like King David and Solomon, Asaph and Aleph—and the reassurances they hold of a God who is near. It comforts me to read words like these:

> Where can I go from your Spirit?
>> Where can I flee from your presence?
> If I go up to the heavens, you are there;
>> if I make my bed in the depths, you are there.
> If I rise on the wings of the dawn,
>> if I settle on the far side of the sea,
> even there your hand will guide me,
>> your right hand will hold me fast. (Ps. 139:7–10 NIV)

Reading about this ever-present God is great—but reading about him is only part of the story. It comforts me to feel God's "even there" presence David described when I long to know I am not alone. It matters that the God who can locate a king, who rises on the wings of the dawn, or who settles on the far side of the sea can find me, driving carpool in the north Atlanta suburbs, just as easily.

Surrender to this God is not a once-for-all, do-it-yourself exercise in self-will. It's an offering that's continually undertaken in the context of relationship. The one I am surrendering myself to is no stranger: he is the God of "Never Stopping, Never Giving Up, Unbreaking, Always and Forever Love,"[1] as *The Jesus Storybook Bible* so beautifully describes him. The heroes of our faith didn't trust this great, good God because they were told they should and they minded—they trusted him because he had shown himself to be great, good, and trustworthy. Not just once—over and over and over again.

There aren't many stories in the Bible that make my heart pound and my pulse race like the story of Abraham and his son Isaac. It brings all my mommy-anxiety racing to the surface and triggers every last fight-or-flight reflex in my body.

Abraham was a man God both knew and made himself known to. God called Abraham away from his homeland, promised him descendants more numerous than the stars in the night sky or the grains of sand on the ocean's shore, and insisted that in old age he and his barren wife, Sarah, would finally become parents of a son. And they did! They became parents of a boy they named Isaac when Abraham was one hundred years old and Sarah almost as old herself!

God told Abraham that through Isaac he would become the father of nations and that God's promises would be passed down through Isaac for generations to come.

The choice of Abraham as a man God would bless and use to bless others wasn't based on Abraham's merit. God chose Abraham because God chose Abraham. Not because he was the most likely candidate in all of Ur to become a great patriarch or because God was certain he would always do the right thing. (Spoiler alert: he didn't, and neither do we—and God is not surprised.) We don't have to worry that he will abandon us when we fail or behave badly, because he didn't choose to love us based on our performance! The relationship we have with him rests entirely on *his* faithfulness and merit—not our own. This is something Abraham would learn in a stunning call to surrender that would make even the strongest man in the world go weak in the knees.

As the story goes, one day God spoke to Abraham and instructed him to do something utterly unthinkable: "Take your son, your only son, whom you love—Isaac—and go to the region of Moriah. Sacrifice him there as a burnt offering on a mountain I will show you" (Gen. 22:2 NIV).

Wait. No. What? Take who?

Take the promised son you gave me, and go where? Sacrifice him to you as what?

As a parent, I can hardly imagine hearing those awful words. It was hard enough for us to surrender Timothy to the surgeon's knife when he was a few months old to repair his cleft lip—and we knew it was for his good. Abraham was being asked to take a knife to his beloved son to kill him!

Shockingly, Abraham obeyed his God, took Isaac, and started out for the place of sacrifice. Maybe more conversation took place between God's command and Abraham's response, but if it did, we're not told about it. God commanded, and Abraham went. Then, at the place God indicated, he bound his son to a makeshift altar and prepared to slay Isaac, his promised heir, the boy that he and Sarah loved.

Here's what happened:

> Then he reached out his hand and took the knife to slay his son. But the angel of the LORD called out to him from heaven, "Abraham! Abraham!"
>
> "Here I am," he replied.
>
> "Do not lay a hand on the boy," he said. "Do not do anything to him. Now I know that you fear God, because you have not withheld from me your son, your only son."
>
> Abraham looked up and there in a thicket he saw a ram caught by its horns. He went over and took the ram and sacrificed it as a burnt offering instead of his son. (Gen. 22:10–13 NIV)

Honestly, my heart struggles with this story. I have a hard time imagining the terrible testing Abraham and Isaac endured and how they could have possibly survived such a thing with their hearts in one piece. But what I do understand is this: Abraham's lived experience of the power and trustworthiness and goodness of God was so great that, as unthinkable as God's command seemed, it was even more unthinkable for him to refuse to obey. To imagine that his own plan was better. To think that surrender to God was the way to death and despair, not to life and hope.

Abraham trusted God, and because he acted on that trust, he experienced in an even deeper and more unforgettable way the "never stopping, never giving up, unbreaking, always and forever love" of his God.

What I'm saying is this: God got plenty personal with Abraham. He gets personal with his people in every age, and he always proves himself trustworthy and faithful in his interactions with us. The God who instructed Abraham to sacrifice his son was the God who provided the very sacrifice he required! We may not understand his ways. We may not always feel comfortable or safe or secure in our obedience. We trust the God we know by personal experience and then pray for the "grace to trust him more" because the only God we can reasonably offer our surrendered life to is the God we know.

A few years back, a craze known as *Frozen* hit our house. The Disney animated movie about a girl named Elsa with some pretty special powers was big, big, big with Josie—and whether you're a parent or not, chances are you've heard Idina Menzel belt out Elsa's theme song, "Let It Go." We heard it plenty, both on the movie video and live—sung with great four-year-old enthusiasm by Josie, wearing her Elsa nightgown with her fine, blond hair falling out of an almost-Elsa braid.

As phenomenal as the song was, I had a tiny problem

with its lyrics: Where was all this "letting it go" going? Let it go . . . to whom? While there are days I would love to just let go of my problems, my responsibilities, my electric bill, and a thousand other things, is that really the answer to my stress and anxiety? And honestly, when circumstances feel more manageable, I'm just as likely to be found singing, "Take it back, take it back" as I am, "Let it go, let it go."

When Elsa belted out "Let it go," she was letting rip her superpower of freezing things—building icy towers and bridges and castles where she would rule and be in charge. But neither the "letting go" of ditching our responsibilities nor the "letting go" of exercising our own brand of personal power and control are the kind of letting go that God desires from us.

His hope for his children is that we will surrender our fears and worries, our guarded assets and our hidden liabilities, our desire for autonomy and our longing for control to him. That we will do what Peter says: cast all our anxieties on him because he cares for us (1 Peter 5:7).

We're not made to grab the controls of our lives with both hands or to fling our worries and anxieties to the far winds with perfectly pitched abandon. Instead we're made to place every aspect of our lives into the very capable hands of our wise, strong, loving Father.

If I believe he is the Creator of the universe, won't he be a reliable keeper of my life? If he was there for me yesterday, won't he be there tomorrow too?

About the time *Frozen* became popular and Josie began singing "Let It Go," I was learning to sing a different song about letting go—one called "I Can Just Be Me." And in this one, there is no mistaking who is being invited to take control:

> I've been holding on so tightly
> To all the things that I think
> Could satisfy my soul
> But I'm letting go . . .
> So be my father, my mighty warrior, be my king.
> 'Cause I can be scattered, frail and shattered,
> Lord, I need You now to be,
> Be my God, so I can just be me.[2]

I can't "let it go" until I'm confident that the one I surrender my life to really is my Father, my mighty Warrior, and my King, and the way I come to know this is by experience. The longer I walk with God, the more certain I become that this is true. The more time I spend in his presence, with his people, and in his Word, the surer I am of his wise and loving care. When I see him for who he is and trust his worth, I don't have to be my own ruler anymore. If my God is worthy, then he is trustworthy too. It's not either/or; it's both/and. Because his track record speaks for itself, with David I can say:

> But I trust in your unfailing love;
> my heart rejoices in your salvation.
> I will sing the LORD's praise,
> for he has been good to me. (Ps. 13:5–6 NIV)

CJ

The life God is calling me to requires living with open hands—trusting him day by day with the smallest of details and the greatest of struggles. He invites each one of his children to embrace this lifestyle of surrender, releasing control to him and believing he is, has always been, and will forever be faithful.

In my role as a worship leader, I am constantly reminding myself that you and I are participants in a glorious story that begins with God and with what he has done. When we begin with our focus on ourselves, we stand on shaky ground, disoriented and unanchored. But when we begin by prizing God for who he is, when we focus on what he has done both throughout history and for us personally—we stand on solid ground, giving him the honor and the glory he deserves.

It's a wonder that the God who created the universe has initiated a relationship with us. He wants to be with us! It's a wonder that he invites us to be a part of his great story. God is not our "buddy" or our life coach, not someone we just enjoy hanging around whose advice is usually pretty good. He's our King.

He deserves our complete trust, obedience, and loyalty. He has earned it. His actions toward us have demonstrated that our God is faithful and true. I want you to see that the object of our worship is 100 percent worthy. Surrendering our lives to him makes sense when we see him for who he is: the God who knows us, loves us, and makes promises to his people that he means to keep. So let's do a deeper dive into those aspects of his character together.

WHITE FLAG PRAYER #3

God, you are good and trustworthy. Thank you for wanting a relationship with me. May my deepest longing be to surrender to your great love and care for me. Amen.

FOUR

A God Who Knows

Remember the kid in school who knew every answer? I was not that kid. I was an average student, not a brilliant one, but I'm pretty sure my parents would tell you I went through a stage when I thought I knew everything. Like almost every teenager breathing, I had ideas about how the world should work, what the rules should be, and even why they didn't always apply to me. But I can tell you now on the far side of puberty that I most certainly did not know everything.

I still don't know it all, but I know someone who does—God. As the Creator of all that was, is, and ever will be, he knows circumstances I don't and sees things I cannot. "Call to me and I will answer you," he invited the prophet Jeremiah, "and tell you great and unsearchable things you do not know" (Jer. 33:3 NIV). There's so much I need to learn!

He knows the deepest corners of my heart, my motives,

my fears, my prejudices, even the ones that are hidden from me. "You have searched me, LORD, and you know me," wrote King David. "You know when I sit and when I rise; you perceive my thoughts from afar. You discern my going out and my lying down; you are familiar with all my ways" (Ps. 139:1–3 NIV). What an incredible comfort to be known this way!

God knows the plans he has for my future. The days to come that are still a mystery to me are an open book to him. "'For I know the plans I have for you,' declares the LORD, 'plans to prosper you and not to harm you, plans to give you hope and a future'" (Jer. 29:11 NIV). I long for the grace to watch his plans unfold!

He knows all these things. I do not. And because he knows, I need to depend on his knowledge and lean on his understanding.

Surrendering to this God who knows is a choice—a choice that rests with me.

I've said before that when Martin and I moved to Atlanta, we didn't think we'd stay for more than the two years it would take him to finish his master's degree. In our minds, we were coming for very practical reasons: I had an opportunity to work full-time for Perimeter Church, which was the perfect scenario for us while Martin studied design and worked part-time. All of our extended family—his and mine—were in the Carolinas, where we grew up, met, went to school, and eventually married. We were excited about the move but felt in our hearts we were "short timers" in

Georgia, at least as far as we knew. But God knew more. He already saw what we couldn't.

We could not have imagined what God had in store for us when Martin was diagnosed, but to say things changed dramatically for us is an understatement. As he moved after his second surgery from intensive care to a step-down unit to a rehab facility, the realization that our lives would never be the same came gradually—but it came. Looking back, this slow dawning was probably a mercy too. The full reality of our situation would have been too overwhelming to take in all at once. God knew that too.

I began to understand that we were going to need help and that we would not be returning to the easy independence we'd enjoyed as newlyweds. When we arrived in Atlanta, we knew one person: John Roland, who had discipled Martin in college. But as Martin began to recover, we found ourselves being woven into a large but tight-knit faith community that we now consider to be one of our greatest blessings. (At this point, they couldn't even pay us to leave!)

For several weeks after Martin was released from rehab, we lived with our senior pastor, Randy Pope, and his wife, Carol, in their newly built mother-in-law suite. Our second-story condo was impossible for us to safely navigate in and out of, and there was no way I could leave Martin alone there, even for a little while. When the Popes opened their home to us, it felt like a big, wide net being moved into place beneath our crazy-scary high-wire act. And even though we'd have been surrounded 24/7 by plenty of caring family and lifelong friends in South Carolina, the neurosurgeon who "wrote the book" on Martin's surgery and saved his life was in Atlanta. (I am positively certain God knew all of this in advance.) Over and over again God met our needs, often before we knew or could even ask for what we needed and always in his perfect time.

Our address wasn't the only thing in our lives that was changing. Clearly, Martin was not returning to school. That was no longer our goal. Our new near-term goal was for him to be able to care for himself—shower, shave, and dress; remember to take his meds; and be safely left alone for short periods of time. And *my* short-term goal—being our very temporary primary breadwinner—was looking more and more like a long-term proposition. I needed to step up my game in the job skills department ASAP. And because God knew that, he had already begun paving the way.

Shortly before Martin's diagnosis, I led music for a retreat in Flat Rock, North Carolina. The speaker that weekend, Jay Sklar, was a professor at Covenant Theological Seminary and a fantastic teacher. At the close of the event, Jay handed me his card and said, "I know seminary isn't for everyone, but if you ever feel God calling you into full-time ministry and want more training, I think Covenant would be a good fit for you." I thanked him, tucked the card away in my Bible, and didn't give it much more thought—until the day Martin and I were getting ready to leave the rehab center. That morning I heard the doctor's final assessment ringing in my ears: "We don't know yet what the extent of your husband's recovery will be. There is a possibility that he will remain on long-term disability." I pulled Jay's card out of my Bible, walked out to the parking lot, and called his number at Covenant.

"I was remembering what you said about training," I

told him. "I think I'm being called to a more full-time ministry than what I imagined before, and I'm pretty sure I'm going to need some of that now."

As you can see, my call to vocational ministry didn't come through a heavenly vision, and it wasn't accompanied by a lot of bells and whistles. It was a call of necessity, pure and simple, but no less spiritual because of that. God knew I would need more study and preparation as he paved the way for me to minister through speaking, singing, teaching, and writing, and the provision for that was already in place by the time I caught up with his plan. (Note for those who think you can get out ahead of him: You can't. Ever. Give up now.)

Perimeter already had a great continuing education program in place for staff, with funding set aside for advanced studies. I began part-time distance studies that same year and received my MA in Theological Studies from Covenant Seminary in 2012—six years after we first arrived in Atlanta. I had planned exactly none of that. Zero.

I can't stress enough that I never, ever saw myself as someone who would pursue an advanced degree. It was just not patterned for me when I was young that a wife would work outside the home, and I didn't imagine that I would either—at least not for long. (Okay, yes, I know that sounds naive and old-fashioned, too, but it's true.) I wasn't a particularly focused undergrad, either, switching majors and schools more than once before finally receiving a degree from a conservative Bible college with an emphasis on music—at age twenty-five. I played in a band the whole time and didn't always take a full load of classes, so I crammed the usual four years into eight.

It's fair to say I graduated from Columbia International University with very little ambition and even less certainty about what kind of job I might pursue. Many of my classmates were heading for the mission field or getting great jobs with churches. I wasn't. I moved back into my parents' home in Spartanburg with no firm plans, and I began to work for my dad, filing medical records for his cardiology practice. If I had taken an inventory of my marketable assets back then, the list would have been woefully short. I hadn't prepared for an obvious career like my physician-father or school teacher-mother. Sure, I could sing, play piano, and write songs my mother thought were great, but songwriting and performing doesn't necessarily translate to income. The relationship with a guy I had dated early in my senior year fizzled, and Martin and I—who were off and on since high school—were more "off" than "on" at the moment. I'm pretty sure I would have gone to Africa if someone had asked, but what I had to offer was apparently not in hot demand there either. I loved God and wanted to serve him, but I had no clue what that should look like. I didn't get what he was doing with my life. But he most definitely had a plan. He always does.

The Bible is full of stories that demonstrate God's providence—his knowing faithfulness. One of my favorites is the story of Ruth. Ruth's story begins and ends in Bethlehem, best known as the birthplace of Christ—but it takes place generations before that historic event. It chronicles a family facing devastating hardship, sorrow, and loss, and it centers around two very strong women. It begins with a famine, but it ends with the one who calls himself the Bread of Life.

Elimelech and Naomi were Jews, living in Bethlehem of Judah when a famine crippled the land. They left Judah for Moab with their two sons, literally looking for greener pastures. They needed food. Moab had plenty. In Moab Elimelech died, leaving Naomi a widow. Her two sons, Mahlon and Chilion, married Moabite women, and the five of them lived together in Moab ten more years. Both wives were childless when Mahlon and Chilion died, too, leaving Naomi and her two daughters-in-law, Orpah and Ruth, to comfort each other.

Naomi learned that "the LORD had paid attention to his people's need" (Ruth 1:6 CSB) in Bethlehem, providing them food again. She decided to return home, and Orpah and Ruth prepared to travel back with her to the land of Judah. She tried to discourage this, reminding them that she had nothing to offer them any more:

> "Go your way, for I am too old to have a husband. If I should say I have hope, even if I should have a husband this night and should bear sons, would you therefore wait till they were grown? Would you therefore refrain from marrying? No, my daughters, for it is exceedingly bitter to me for your sake that the hand of the LORD has gone out against me." (Ruth 1:12–13 ESV)

Before you decide Naomi was having an unnecessary pity party, remember this: in her culture, she *was* lost. She had no husband, no sons, and no heirs to care for her. She really was a woman who had lost everything. She was telling her daughters-in-law, "Don't bet on me. You'll lose. I have nothing for myself and nothing for you." She had no plan for prosperity in Bethlehem, but she had nowhere else to go either. And it seemed as if God had forgotten her.

Orpah listened to reason. She returned to her homeland, but Ruth refused. In some of the most beautiful language of Scripture, she pledged her loyalty to Naomi:

> "Do not urge me to leave you or to return from following you. For where you go I will go, and where you lodge I will lodge. Your people shall be my people, and your God my God. Where you die I will die, and there will I be buried. May the LORD do so to me and more also if anything but death parts me from you." (vv. 16–17 ESV)

Ruth went all in. She was going with Naomi and identifying herself with Naomi's God. It didn't seem to make sense, but she called on the name of *Yahweh*, a proper name for God built on the Hebrew word for "I AM." That name evokes all of God's power, constancy, goodness, truth, and beauty. Ruth would eventually see his character demonstrated, even in the midst of sorrow and desperate poverty—but she couldn't see it yet. She was moving forward in faith.

When the two women arrived in Bethlehem, the locals hardly recognized Naomi. The years had been hard on her. And while Ruth had decided to place her trust in Naomi's God, Naomi believed that same God had turned against her:

> "Do not call me Naomi; call me Mara, for the Almighty has dealt very bitterly with me. I went away full, and the

LORD has brought me back empty. Why call me Naomi, when the LORD has testified against me and the Almighty has brought calamity upon me?" (Ruth 1:20–21 ESV)

Naomi wasn't putting on a happy face, and she wasn't pulling any punches. She saw God as 100 percent responsible for her circumstances, and her circumstances were not good. Can you relate? If we are God's children, if we are trusting him and by no fault of our own we find ourselves in pain, isn't he responsible? And if we are hurting, isn't that likely proof that we've been abandoned—that God has somehow turned against us or forgotten us? Naomi thought so and said so. But the first chapter of Ruth ends with a sentence so heavy with promise you can almost feel the scales beginning to tip back to plenty: "They came to Bethlehem at the beginning of barley harvest" (v. 22 ESV).

The series of events that unfolds next for Naomi and Ruth would seem unbelievable—except for the God who knows. Ruth went to the barley fields to glean, and she just "happened" to land in the field that belonged to Boaz, who just "happened" to be a distant relative of Naomi's husband, Elimelech. Boaz just "happened" to take notice of Ruth, inquired about her, and invited her to stay in his field, close to his female servants. Ruth was stunned by the kindness of Boaz and asked why he was so good to her, a foreigner. His answer was simple and straightforward:

"All that you have done for your mother-in-law since the death of your husband has been fully told to me, and how you left your father and mother and your native land and

came to a people that you did not know before. The LORD
repay you for what you have done, and a full reward be
given you by the LORD, the God of Israel, under whose
wings you have come to take refuge!" (Ruth 2:11–12 ESV)

Kind words, for sure. But Boaz's kindness didn't stop
with words. He ordered his workmen to let Ruth gather
grain not just at the edges of the field but among the stalks
the harvesters had cut. "Don't humiliate her," he told them.
"Pull out some stalks from the bundles for her and leave
them for her to gather" (vv. 15–16 CSB). He made provision
not just for her hunger but also for her dignity. And at the
end of the day, Ruth went home with twenty-six quarts of
grain! Naomi was amazed at her daughter-in-law's "glean-
ings" and asked where she gathered them. When Ruth said
all of it came from the field of Boaz, a light finally went on
for Naomi:

> "May he be blessed by the LORD, whose kindness has not
> forsaken the living or the dead!" Naomi also said to her,
> "The man is a close relative of ours, one of our redeem-
> ers." (v. 20 ESV)

When she returned to Bethlehem, Naomi believed that
God had forgotten her. But he never did. He went ahead and
prepared a blessing for her and for her daughter-in-law. Now
she could see his hand where it was invisible before. Boaz
was their kin and could redeem this family from hopelessness and despair. He could offer them a future and a hope.
And he was ready to do just that.

Naomi encouraged Ruth to place herself at Boaz's feet and to privately invite him to redeem her—to marry her, in other words—and keep all that had once been Elimelech's in the family. As crazy as this plan sounds to our Western ears, Ruth moved forward in faith again and did as Naomi said. Boaz honored Ruth's trust and was all too happy to make her his wife. He promised to marry her, to care for the property of Elimelech in his name, and to keep the family legacy alive. In other words, all that Naomi believed to be lost was restored through Ruth and Boaz. She would be cared for in her old age. She would have a home in her land for the rest of her life. She would have a family again.

But the story doesn't end there. Ruth and Boaz didn't just live happily ever after. Oh no. They had a child together, a son they named Obed. He was the joy of Naomi's old age, and she took good care of him. Then Obed had a son named Jesse, who had a son named David. (Yes, that David!) And if we turn forward to the gospel of Matthew,[1] we learn that through Obed's grandson David, twenty-eight generations later, Jesus Christ was born to Mary and Joseph in Bethlehem, the City of Bread, where Ruth gleaned all those years ago!

Who knew? God knew!

All those things that just "happened" to Naomi and Ruth weren't coincidences. Not by a long shot. God was at work behind the scenes, making a way to provide for the needs of these two women and, at the same time, making a way for his Son to provide for the needs of the world. What looked like an impossible situation wasn't. What looked like tragedy held a powerful blessing in store. Naomi couldn't have planned it. Ruth couldn't have either. They were unknowing participants in God's plan, a plan that was in place before the first famine ever hit Judah. God knew what Naomi needed. He knew what Ruth needed. He knew Boaz's whereabouts and his heart. He knew.

When I wonder if God knows my needs, the story of Ruth reminds me that he does. When I imagine that I've been overlooked or forgotten by God, I remember how Naomi's lament turned to praise. When I think I can see the outcome ahead and I'm afraid that it's not good, I tell myself that this same God is at work in my life, too, and that he means to benefit me. I don't have to work like crazy to make sure all the pieces fit. The story is not mine to write. It's his.

There's one more thing I need to tell you about this God who knows and about why we should surrender our lives to him: he's tender. He doesn't taunt us with his superior understanding or punish us for not seeing in advance what he sees. His knowing is not a haughty, arrogant knowing. It's not puffed up and proud, like human knowledge can be. It is full of tender, pursuing love. It's personal. We sometimes accuse God of being indifferent, late to the party, aloof, or unkind. But he is none of these. He doesn't just know all things—he knows us. He knows our love language. He knows our deepest desires. He knows what's best for us, and when.

Martin and I reconnected a short time after I moved back home to Spartanburg from college, and we began dating again. I was playing guitar for his college ministry every Monday night, packing forty or more kids into his tiny house. He'd teach, and I'd play. It was the sweetest, simplest thing. I was exploring a solo music career at the same time, and a record company in Nashville had expressed interest in me. We'd signed a form of intent, and a long-form contract was under way. I thought it was a done deal and imagined that this must be God's will for my life—at least for the next few years of it. But plans sure can change.

The record company I was negotiating with merged with another label, and the president I had been talking to at one label was suddenly the vice president of another. I was invited in to talk to "the new guy" and clearly didn't realize what was on the line. I'm almost embarrassed to say this now, but I showed up for that meeting in burlap overalls and a white tank top, fresh from a hike. And when I say fresh, I mean *fresh*. I don't think I'd showered that day, and maybe not even the day before. We had the "where do you see yourself in five years" conversation, at a time when I could barely see into the next week!

You can probably guess where this was going: they pulled the contract. I thought I was moving to Nashville to be the next Jaci Velasquez. They thought I needed more ambition—and better hygiene! It was sad but also clarifying. I had wondered how I was going to continue dating Martin from a distance and how our relationship would be affected if I moved. It turns out I didn't have to worry about either of those things. I wasn't leaving.

As we continued to date, Martin and I began to talk about marriage. I felt certain a proposal was coming any minute, and I thought I knew when. We were planning a weekend at the beach, driving down to Charleston with my parents. I knew Martin already had the ring; I'd rounded a corner at the house one day and seen him showing it to my mom.

The night we arrived, he said, "I'd like for us to take a walk out on the dock."

"Sure," I told him. This was it. I knew this was it.

Then my dad said, "Let's all play Scrabble!" And Martin *agreed*. I couldn't believe it. I was dying to get out the door and down to the dock and get that ring on my finger, and now we were going to play a stupid board game with my parents! That game seemed to last forever, and when it was finally over I could barely keep my eyes open. We hadn't cleared all the tiles from the board before Martin said, "Let's play again!"

Are. You. Kidding. Me?

"I'm tired," I announced (and probably not too sweetly). "Y'all can play. I'm going to bed."

I was more than a little mad, but knowing Martin, it wasn't unreasonable to think that he was just playing with me—that he was going to surprise me in the middle of the night with the ring. So I put on my cutest pajamas, brushed my teeth and my hair, and laid down in my bed . . . where I waited all night long for him to knock on my door with a proposal. He didn't. I mean, I hardly slept a wink.

The next morning at breakfast, Martin seemed completely oblivious to how he'd messed up the plan. "Good morning," he said, so cheerful I wanted to throw a biscuit at him. "How did you sleep?" *How did I sleep? Are you kidding me? I didn't. I waited all night for you to come and ask me to marry you.* But I said nothing. I was determined to keep my mouth shut and wait for his timing. He obviously had something else planned for the weekend, right? But we were at the beach for three days, and I never saw that ring. Finally, I couldn't take it anymore. On Monday I let him have it.

"I know you picked up the ring in Columbia," I said. "I know you showed it to my mom, and I don't understand what is going on."

"Laura," he said. "I could propose to you right now. But I'm going to ask you to trust me. Would you just trust me?"

Two days later, on Wednesday, I woke up to rose petals in my bed and a note from Martin that said, "I have the most extraordinary day planned for you." And he did. *Because he knows me.* We began the day in Spartanburg, in our favorite park. Then we got coffee from our favorite coffee shop. That evening, Martin had great tickets for *Les Misérables*, my all-time favorite musical. I mean, the day could not have been more perfect. Except it was. After the show we headed for a coffee shop in Greenville, where Martin had heard me play so many times through the years. They were closed when we arrived, but he'd gotten the key from the owner and filled it with candles, all glowing. He had the ring. He asked the question. And I said yes.

My sweet husband didn't just plan a moment for me. He planned a day filled with moments he knew I would love and with reminders of memories we'd made together. It was perfect because he knows me and he knows what makes my heart full. It was better than the dock after a family Scrabble game. (I would have been too irritated then to really enjoy it!) His timing wasn't my timing, but his timing was good. And God's is too.

I can trust my heavenly Father to do what's right for me. I can trust his timing. I can trust his love and be confident in his provision, not just because he knows all circumstances and he knows the future but also because he knows—and loves—me. And you can trust him too.

WHITE FLAG PRAYER #4

God, you know me and are always working for my good. Show me the wisdom of staying in step with your Spirit instead of jumping ahead on my own. Amen.

FIVE

A God Who Loves Me

I'm a married woman with four children, but some of my closest friends are single. When I get annoyed at Martin over stray socks on the bathroom floor, or when the twins have a stomach virus at the same time and there are no clean clothes left to put on them, I imagine the blissful freedom of the unencumbered life—and my single friends are quick to jerk me back to reality! While they are wondering where all the good guys went or lamenting their last bad blind date, I can invite them over to casa Elvington, where they can see that marriage is no fairy tale, that domestic bliss is fleeting at best, and that having a partner is a good thing, yes, but it's no guarantee of lifelong security or unending joy. (Come to think of it, unending joy this side of heaven is a myth, too, whether you're married *or* single.)

One question I am often asked when I talk with single women is, "How can I be sure this guy really cares for me?"

Women might spend hours trying to suss out the hidden meaning of a guy's offhand comment, hoping to figure out what he might have meant by a stray "yes" or "uh" or "maybe." But I've learned actions are a far, far better gauge of someone's meaning or intention than words could ever be. My best advice is, instead of trying to figure out what a guy means by his words, study what his actions are telling you. Because at the end of the day, love isn't just something you say; love is something you *do*.

When I was anticipating a proposal from Martin and waiting to hear the words, "Laura Story, will you marry me?" a tiny part of me might have believed the *words* I was waiting for would prove Martin's love and his commitment. But what he intended to do—and did—was demonstrate his love for me by creating a day full of the things I loved, honoring the memories we'd already made together. His actions that day spoke his intentions loud and clear: *I see you, Laura. I know you. I treasure you. I mean to keep on loving you this way as long as we both live.*

Are there days, fifteen years later, when one or the other of us doesn't *feel* particularly loving? Sure, there are. But that doesn't erase the years of blessings we've shared or the sacrifices we've made for each other—or prevent us from choosing to love one another all over again. Again, love is something you do, not just something you say.

Because we're human, we may question the depth of our love for another person (or theirs for us), but we have no reason to wonder how God feels about us. Not ever. He's simply given us too much hard evidence to doubt his love. So if we're debating whether or not it's wise or safe to surrender control of our lives to him, we need to remind ourselves not just how well he knows us but how well he's already loved us. And not just with words—with actions.

Paul wrote in Romans of an historical act by the Son of God that speaks volumes about the depth of the Father's love for us:

> You see, at just the right time, when we were still power-less, Christ died for the ungodly. Very rarely will anyone die for a righteous person, though for a good person someone might possibly dare to die. But God demon-strates his own love for us in this: While we were still sinners, Christ died for us. (Rom. 5:6–8 NIV)

The love of God, Paul said, is demonstrated beyond a doubt by the once-for-all sacrificial death of Christ. The crucifixion is the last word on love. The mic drop. The end-all, be-all. The irrefutable proof. It *would* be extremely rare for anyone to offer to die for another person, even a righteous or good one. But someone *did* die for love. And so that we're not confused about whether we might have deserved that kind of love, Paul is brutally blunt: we did not. We were powerless, ungodly sinners when God poured out his love on us. He loved us out of the perfection of his heart, in spite of the obvious flaws of our own.

Why is this such good news? Because it means God's love for me rests on God's character, not mine. On God's goodness, not my own. On God's strong, pursuing love, not my weak, wavering imitation of it. If I didn't earn his love by my good behavior, I won't lose it when I behave badly—and sometimes I do. When I place my faith in the finished work of Christ's death and resurrection, I am on solid ground with God. His love for me is not iffy. Listen to what Tim Keller says about this great, good news: "The gospel is this: We are more sinful and flawed in ourselves than we ever dared believe, yet at the very same time we are more loved and accepted in Jesus Christ than we ever dared hope."[1]

And really, how good is that? It's uncontestable that he loves us! The strongest feelings of love I have look like apathy compared to the amazing demonstration of God's love for me in Jesus.

One of the first Bible verses most Christians learn is John 3:16: "For God so loved the world that he gave his one and only Son, that whoever believes in him shall not perish but have eternal life" (NIV). This gospel-in-a-nutshell sounds global and all-encompassing doesn't it? I mean, we're talking about the whole world here. But "whoever believes" is personal. Belief is not a group project. We come to believe as individuals. One by one. God loves us with this great big pursuing love, demonstrates he means business by giving his only Son to die in our place, and invites us to personally respond to that love with simple belief that he is who he says he is. That he's done what only he could do. That the love of God in Christ is the one and only thing that will save us from the deadly consequences of our own sin—a sin we can't get rid of without serious, supernatural help. And that his amazing love is ours for the asking.

This kind of love is so different from what passes for love today! Our idea of love has been hijacked by the candy-sweet stuff of romance novels or Hallmark movies or—heaven help us!—by "reality" shows like *The Bachelor* or *The Bachelorette*. Friend, God didn't give you his first rose, or his final one. He gave you his Son! He didn't put your love for him to the test; he went to the cross to prove his love for you!

He's not checking out our online profiles or trying us out on group dates to see which of us will shine. Nor is he teasing us with the promise of one-on-ones before rejecting us for someone more likely to please him. No! He's decided to love us, and he loved us *first*. He's put everything on the line to bring us together forever. The story of God's love is that his heart was broken for me and for you so that whatever broken-heartedness we walk through will only be a faint reflection of what he endured for us. It sounds too good to be true, I know, but it is real!

"Greater love has no one than this," wrote the apostle John, "to lay down one's life for one's friends" (John 15:13 NIV). I don't know that I'll ever get over the fact that Jesus gave his life for me:

I was found
As a beggar, as an orphan with no home
No family
I was found
With a stain as deep as darkness fills the night
But the wonder does not lie in the depression of my state
But that You found me at all is simply grace upon grace . . .
And now I find

That the comforts of this heart are not in things
Or in the joys that this life brings
But just to be
The reworkmanship of God to know He's with me
To know He's for me
And I can't begin to comprehend just why He's chosen me
But I'd spend a thousand lifetimes giving thanks
Giving You thanks[2]

You and I are loved relentlessly by a God who was willing to spend everything on our behalf and who is reworking
those of us who believe into the perfect image of his beautiful
Son. In Jesus we are given the ultimate happily-ever-after,
but it begins here and now. We don't have to wait for heaven
to experience being secure in God's love. God has made a
way for us to experience his love in our ordinary, everyday
lives. Again, Paul let us in on the secret of how that works:

> I pray that out of his glorious riches he may strengthen
> you with power through his Spirit in your inner being, so
> that Christ may dwell in your hearts through faith. And I
> pray that you, being rooted and established in love, may
> have power, together with all the Lord's holy people, to
> grasp how wide and long and high and deep is the love of
> Christ, and to know this love that surpasses knowledge—
> that you may be filled to the measure of all the fullness of
> God. (Eph. 3:16–19 NIV)

Have you ever gotten a gift that was too big for you?
Something that you had to grow into, like a shiny two-wheel

bike or a two-sizes-too-big winter coat? Probably the gift came from someone who loved you, someone who knew what size you were but who rightly believed you'd grow. Someone confident that you had inside yourself all you needed (along with time) to make that gift fully your own, 100 percent useful and enjoyable.

Well, the love of God is a too-big gift for all of us. It's not easy to take in. We need something beyond ourselves to help us grow up in faith and experience it more fully. And God gives us that too. He gives us his Holy Spirit to live in our hearts, "translating" his giant love in ways that help us to truly "get" it. He makes his love real to us, and he keeps it real. Then, rooted and established in his love, we grow more and more confident in it—and more and more able to grasp its width and height and depth. It's a love that goes beyond knowledge and fills us up.

In one of my favorite moments in C. S. Lewis's The Chronicles of Narnia, Lucy meets up with Aslan the great lion again, after having been away from Narnia for a long while.

> "Aslan," said Lucy, "you're bigger."
> "That's because you are older, little one," answered he.
> "Not because you are?"
> "I am not. But every year you grow, you will find me bigger."[3]

As we grow in our faith, the Holy Spirit enables us to know more and more of God and his love. We receive the power, by his grace and together with his people, to grasp that love. We will have dry times and mountaintop moments. Our feelings will grow strong and then waver. But if you are doubting, if you are going through a season of not feeling God's love or his presence, there is no need to panic. You will also find him "bigger" as you spend time in his presence, as you fill your heart and mind with his Word, and as you gather together with his people.

I'm geared toward the tangible. Maybe you are too. These are things you can actively do to recognize and receive his love afresh: Show up. Be with other believers. Read and study his promises to you and remind yourself of the gospel story—often.

When Martin Luther, the great reformer, preached to the parishioners in the German village of Wittenberg, it is said that he was often accused by them of preaching the same old message, week after week. "I will stop preaching the gospel," he told them, "when you no longer have need of hearing it." (Like, never.) Can the story ever get old? Can we ever *not* need to be reminded of the height, the depth, and the breadth of God's love for us, demonstrated on the cross of Jesus Christ? As often as you can, put yourself in a position to be reminded that "God demonstrates his own love for us in this: While we were still sinners, Christ died for us" (Rom. 5:8 NIV).

Before we leave this subject, I want to address a common misunderstanding about God's love for us. We imagine it's made of the same stuff as our love for him. It's not.

Sometimes we are faithless, even when our intentions are good. But there is never a gap between God's love and the expression of it—even if his timing sometimes disappoints us. He is always faithful to us. He can't be anything else. That's just who he is.

Peter learned this truth the hard way. He'd followed Jesus from the beginning. He'd witnessed the miracles. Heard the powerful teaching. Peter understood Jesus' true identity as the Messiah, the Son of God. He believed in him, and he loved him. So when Jesus began to talk about being betrayed and tried and crucified in Jerusalem, Peter wasn't having any of it. He wasn't ready to lose his friend, and he did not believe anyone who knew Jesus could ever betray him. And he said so: "'No!' Peter insisted. 'Even if I have to die with you, I will never deny you!' And all the other disciples vowed the same" (Matt. 26:35 NLT).

You probably know the rest of the story. When things got dicey, when Jesus was being tried before Caiaphas the high priest and Peter was lurking in the courtyard nearby, he was recognized. Three times he was asked if he was with Jesus, knew Jesus, was a follower of Jesus. He denied it. Three times. The love he felt for Jesus never died, but it didn't translate into action. He was afraid, and he pretended not to know his Lord to save his own skin. If you read the story in the gospel of Luke, you'll come across what has got to be one of the saddest scenes in all of Scripture:

Just as he was speaking, the rooster crowed. The Lord turned and looked straight at Peter. Then Peter remembered the word the Lord had spoken to him: "Before the

rooster crows today, you will disown me three times." And
he went outside and wept bitterly. (Luke 22:60–62 NIV)

Our love is human. God's love is divine. Ours is imperfect. His is perfect. Ours doesn't always translate into action
on our beloved's behalf—but his does.

If the story ended there, it would be heartbreaking. But
it doesn't. After Jesus was raised from the dead, he and
Peter met again—in a familiar place, by the shore of the
Sea of Galilee. Over a meal of roasted fish and bread, they
had a chance to talk. Peter must have remembered that
night and the look that he and Jesus shared, and he must
have felt so ashamed! He'd denied his Savior publicly after
he'd boasted that he would die for him. But Jesus' love for
Peter never wavered. He gave him a make-up quiz (more
for Peter's sake than his own), and this time Peter showed
more promise.

Three times Jesus asked if Peter loved him, and three
times Peter insisted that he did. Three denials. Then three
professions of love. Peter must have been smarting a little
from the third question and answered for the last time,
"Lord, you know all things; you know that I love you" (John
21:17 NIV).

Then Jesus said two more things to his wavering disciple:
"feed my sheep" and "follow me" (vv. 17, 19). Done. Restored.
Forgiven. Reconciled. Invited into relationship and given
another chance to serve.

God's love is so not like ours. It's stronger. Better.
More reliable. It's made of different stuff than our human,
sometimes-weak love for him. His is a love that would go

to any length to restore us and to keep us close to him. We can count on that.

Ↄ

Think of the strongest love you've ever felt for another person. Multiply it by a million, and then a million more. You're still not even close to imagining how much God loves you. How can you be sure? Because of his action on your behalf. Because of the cross. And because the Holy Spirit helps you to experience God's love poured out within your heart and reminds you of just how wide and high and deep it really is.

Ↄ

A few years ago, around Easter time, a friend gave Josie a little glass snow globe. She loved it, but she was really too small to play with it safely—so we set it on the mantle in our living room and shook it for her when she asked us to so she could watch it "snow." She must have asked me several days in a row if she could keep it in her room, and against my better judgment, I finally gave in. "You can look at," I told her, "but Mommy doesn't want you to touch it or hold it."

It didn't take five minutes for me to realize I should have gone with my gut. Seconds after I walked away, I heard the snow globe crash against the dresser, and I knew that it had shattered. I went back to her room, scooped her up and put her in her crib, then started cleaning up the damage. *She's just like me,* I thought. *She makes messes she's not quite big enough to clean up.* But because I love her, I'm willing to step in and do the dirty work. And I wouldn't have it any other way.

After I found the biggest pieces and blotted up the water and "snow," I thought of her toddling on the carpet on her little feet or playing there on her hands and knees. What if there were still tinier pieces I couldn't see? How would I find them? I decided the best way was to get down on the floor myself and press my hands into the rug to try and feel them. I wanted the glass to stick to *my* hands so it wouldn't cut her hands or feet. She had disobeyed me, and I had better things to do with my evening than look for broken glass the hard way, but that little girl is my delight, so I chose to absorb the wounds instead of her. I didn't even have to think twice.

Friend, your God loves you so much that he gave his life for you. He didn't even have to think twice. He wants nothing but what's best for you, and he's more than worthy of your trust. Surrendering to him is no risk at all when you consider the height and depth and breadth of his love:

Do you think anyone is going to be able to drive a wedge between us and Christ's love for us? There is no way! Not trouble, not hard times, not hatred, not hunger, not homelessness, not bullying threats, not backstabbing, not even the worst sins listed in Scripture. . . .

None of this fazes us because Jesus loves us. I'm absolutely convinced that nothing—nothing living or dead, angelic or demonic, today or tomorrow, high or low, thinkable or unthinkable—absolutely *nothing* can get between us and God's love because of the way that Jesus our Master has embraced us. (Rom. 8:35–39 THE MESSAGE)

I'm putting my full weight down on this: you can be absolutely confident of God's love for you. Trust it. Rely on it. Depend on it. Nothing—absolutely nothing—can get between you and the love of God, demonstrated by the cross of Christ.

WHITE FLAG PRAYER #5

Thank you, Father, for loving me based on who you are and not on my worthiness or performance. Help me to love others in the same agenda-free way. Amen.

SIX

A God Who Keeps His Promises

There's just something about love that seems to want to make promises, isn't there? Secular pop music aims plenty of heartfelt "I wills" at the object of a singer's romantic affections, from Dolly Parton's "I Will Always Love You" to John Legend's "All of Me." Inspirational music makes more than its share of promises, too, pledging to God the devotion, obedience, and love he deserves in beautiful hymns and praise songs like "I Am Thine, O Lord," "I Will Worship," and "I Will Follow."

Do you notice a recurring theme in these songs I've just mentioned? I'll give you a hint: look for the pronouns *I* and *me*. In each case, the singer is declaring his or her intent to the beloved one, whether it be a person or God. The singers are the ones making the promises. If you'll allow me another Disney reference (considering my present vocation of mom-in-chief, it may or may not be the last), consider the dilemma of the Beast when he's falling in love with Belle in *Beauty and the Beast.* He's longing to find a way to express his emotions, so he asks his friends for suggestions on ways to win her heart.

"I've never felt this way for anyone," he confesses to Cogsworth and Lumière. "I want to do something for her, but what?"

Cogsworth's quick reply always gets a good laugh from adults who may be watching along with their kids: "Well, there's the usual things: flowers, chocolates, promises you don't intend to keep . . ." We've all been there, right? When our hearts are full, we feel compelled to make bold, sweeping promises, but we're not always good at keeping them! They sound wonderful in the moment, sure, but when reality sets in we need more than just emotion to make them stick.

It's the nature of love to want to promise. Because God *is* love, he makes promises to those he loves. But unlike you and me, he means to keep his promises, and he does.

You don't have to read very far into the Bible to get the idea that we have a promise-making, promise-keeping God. In the garden of Eden, God promised Adam that he would provide food for him from all the beautiful plants and vines and trees he's created, and he did. When Adam came to the end of the animal parade and saw no "helper" suitable for him, God promised to make him one, and he did. From Adam's rib God made Eve and presented her to Adam, who said, "This at last is bone of my bones and flesh of my flesh" (Gen. 2:23 ESV). Or, as we say in the South, "Woo hoo!" God was as good as his word.

He made a specific, conditional promise to Adam:

> You may surely eat of every tree of the garden, but of the tree of the knowledge of good and evil you shall not eat, for in the day that you eat of it you shall surely die. (Gen. 2:16–17 ESV)

The first couple would remain in perfect relationship with God and with each other and flourish forever if only they obeyed him. But they didn't. When Adam and Eve disobeyed God and ate fruit from the one tree he'd forbidden, their eyes were opened, and they became self-aware and ashamed. Spiritual and physical death followed, just as God said they would.

God banished them from the garden, and although they would still "be fruitful and multiply," they would know no end of trouble and disunity for it. In spite of their failure to keep their part of the covenant, God said he would strike Satan's head through Eve's offspring—promising to one day deal a death blow to Satan through Christ and reverse the curse of sin. And God did. Jesus was the promised offspring, and the cross was his death blow.

While the word *covenant* is not introduced in Genesis until chapter 6, the elements of covenant relationship—parties, conditions, promises, and warnings—are there from the very beginning. Adam and Eve forwent God's promise of blessing by disobeying his warning, and through the fall, sin entered the world. But God kept his promises even when Adam and Eve, representing all of us, broke theirs.

From the days of Adam to the time of King David, God reiterated his covenant promises to his people. He made covenants with Noah, with Abraham, with Moses, and with David. Through David, God's final, perfect covenant—the new covenant—would come to all. I'll have more to say about that promise later, but for now, let's consider a very obvious but important part of each of these promises from God: timing.

By the time Noah was born, "the wickedness of man was great in the earth, and . . . every intention of the thoughts of his heart was only evil continually" (Gen. 6:5 ESV). Seeing this, God resolved to wipe mankind from the face of the earth, but he decided to spare Noah and his family. God told Noah he planned to send a great flood and instructed him to build an ark to save himself and his family from the devastation to come. "I will establish my covenant with you," he told Noah, "and you shall come into the ark, you, your sons, your wife, and your sons' wives with you" (v. 18 ESV). Noah did as God instructed, and God brought the Flood. But he preserved the lives of Noah and his family just as he promised.

When Mr. and Mrs. Noah and their brood emerged from the ark, the world was changed, but God promised them that he would never again destroy all life with a flood. As a sign of this, he offered a rainbow, and he told Noah what it meant:

> "I establish my covenant with you, that never again shall
> all flesh be cut off by the waters of the flood, and never

again shall there be a flood to destroy the earth." And God said, "This is the sign of the covenant that I make between me and you and every living creature that is with you, for all future generations: I have set my bow in the cloud, and it shall be a sign of the covenant between me and the earth." (Gen. 9:11–13 ESV)

God has kept this promise too.

Generations after Noah, God reached out to Abraham and made another covenant. Do you notice that God initiated all of these covenants? And do you see how they built upon one another? He was always the one making the overture, establishing the promise. God told Abraham to leave his homeland of Ur and travel to another (yet nameless) place. Then he promised:

> "And I will make of you a great nation, and I will bless you and make your name great, so that you will be a blessing. I will bless those who bless you, and him who dishonors you I will curse, and in you all the families of the earth shall be blessed." (Gen. 12:2–3 ESV)

God's command to Abraham was simple: *go.* His promise to Abraham was threefold: he would give him many descendants (at this time, Abraham and his wife, Sarah, were elderly and childless), he would give them a land of their own (not yet identified), and he would make them and their offspring a blessing to all humankind. God kept every one of these promises, even though Abraham turned out to be a pretty imperfect covenant partner. Through Abraham, a line was established that led directly to Jesus, the Messiah, who would deliver God's people from sin's curse once and for all.

Do you see how important covenant making and covenant keeping is to God's story? How faithful he has always been to his people? How his love compels him to make promises to them—promises he has established a perfect record of keeping?

When Abraham's grandson Jacob moved his entire family to Egypt, Abraham's descendants still numbered less than one hundred. (While I'm here, let me just stop and encourage you to read the entire book of Genesis. Trust me, you want the details!) When they were led out of Egypt centuries later by a God-commissioned man named Moses, they were a great nation just as God said they would be. And the covenant God made with Abraham, he continued through Moses:

> I am the LORD, and I will bring you out from under the burdens of the Egyptians, and I will deliver you from slavery to them, and I will redeem you with an outstretched arm and with great acts of judgment. I will take you to be my people, and I will be your God, and you shall know that I am the LORD your God, who has brought you out from under the burdens of the Egyptians. I will bring you into the land that I swore to give to Abraham, to Isaac, and to Jacob. I will give it to you for a possession. I am the LORD. (Ex. 6:6–8 ESV)

Do I have to tell you that God kept these promises too? He did bring his people out of Egypt—in spectacular ways—and he did redeem them with powerful acts of judgment. They became a weak and whining nation wandering in the wilderness, but God didn't abandon them there either. He had already promised that they were his people and that he was their God. So he led them through the desert step by step, mile by mile, with a pillar of fire at night and a cloud during the day. He fed them with stuff called manna that fell from heaven every morning, just enough for each day. He even persevered with them when they began to complain that they were homesick for Egypt—the very place he'd delivered them out of!

And in the midst of this, God made yet another covenant with his people. This time he gave them laws, and he promised to bless them in return for keeping them. We know these laws as the Ten Commandments, but they're also called the Mosaic covenant or the "old" covenant (because God would establish a new one through Jesus). But even this Mosaic covenant was less a ledger of dos and don'ts than it was a picture of what the love of a holy God should look like. The goal was never performance. The goal was always—in this and every covenant—relationship.

It doesn't take a rocket scientist to predict the outcome of this agreement: God's people had a hard time holding up their end. But again, even though this covenant was a conditional one, God's loving-kindness toward them never wavered. His people experienced the consequences of their rebellion and disobedience alright, but his love for them always remained strong. He never disowned them, even when they faced his discipline. We don't do that with our children either, right? We may correct them all day long, but we still feed them, kiss them, and tuck them in at night. Because family is family.

After God's people wandered in the desert for forty years, he gave them the land he promised to Abraham. Every step of the way he led them into the fulfillment of his promises, even when they seemed determined to forfeit his blessing by doing it their own way. Does any of this ring a bell? Do you ever identify with the Israelites? I do. I doubt, at times, that God's intentions toward me are good. I question his timing. I wonder if my poor performance will keep him from acting on my behalf, or I imagine that my "good" works will somehow encourage him to act sooner. I fail to understand that his faithfulness doesn't rely on my faith—not even a little bit.

Even though the Israelites ratified the Mosaic covenant by insisting they were going all in for God, they didn't. Not really. They spiraled through cycle after cycle of faith, doubt, unbelief, sin, repentance, faith, and doubt, in a kind of Old Testament version of *Groundhog Day*. They were serially unfaithful to God, while he was consistently faithful to them.

Eventually, they forgot their commitment to their covenant-making God altogether and "served the Baals and the Asheroth"—the foreign gods of neighboring lands—instead (Judg. 3:7 ESV). "Everyone did what was right in his own eyes" (Judg. 17:6 ESV) in those days, in spite of the warnings of a slew of prophets and judges sent by God. It was a dark time for God's people, maybe not too different in some ways from today. Not surprisingly, the Israelites did what we sometimes do when things look bleak: they decided they needed new leadership when what they really needed was a renewed heart.

The people begged for a king, and God gave them a warrior named Saul. He looked good—straight from central casting, you might say—but the reign of Saul ended badly. While Saul was still king, God chose his successor, an unlikely young shepherd boy named David who had a very thin résumé—except for one storied dustup with a Philistine giant named Goliath. Through David, not Saul, God made another covenant with his people. David wasn't perfect, not by a long shot, but God called him "a man after my heart, who will do all my will" (Acts 13:22 ESV).

God's covenant with David was a lot like his covenant with Abraham. It was unconditional, for one thing; it tied Israel's destiny to a specific place, and it promised redemption of the people through the family line of David, who also happened to be a descendent of Abraham. Like all of God's covenants that came before, it demonstrated his great loving-kindness and was full of "I wills":

And *I will* make for you a name, like the name of the great ones of the earth. And *I will* appoint a place for my people Israel and will plant them, that they may dwell in their own place and be disturbed no more. And violent men shall waste them no more, as formerly, from the time that I appointed judges over my people Israel. And *I will* subdue all your enemies. Moreover, I declare to you that *the* LORD *will* build you a house. When your days are fulfilled to walk with your fathers, *I will* raise up your offspring after you, one of your own sons, and *I will* establish his kingdom. He shall build a house for me, and *I will* establish his throne forever. *I will* be to him a father, and he shall be to me a son. *I will* not take my steadfast love from him, as I took it from him who was before you, but *I will* confirm him in my house and in my kingdom forever, and his throne shall be established forever. (1 Chron. 17:8–14 ESV, emphasis added)

If God promised and then immediately made good on his promise, and if he instantly acted that way every single time with no waiting, we'd be fantastic followers, wouldn't we? Except a gap almost always exists between the promise and the fulfillment of that promise. I'd go so far as to say the essence of any promise is found in the faith and hope required to keep on believing it. A promise always involves waiting and some degree of anticipation. It's in that space between "I will" and "I have" that relationships are tested and faith is strengthened.

Think about marriage vows. Those of us who are married said those vows to our mate on our wedding day in theory, not out of a vast wealth of experience. Nothing we vowed had been road tested yet. Our love for each other prompted us to make promises in faith on a day when we were full of dreams and looking our very best. We hadn't been poor together yet. Or sick. (Maybe.) Mostly we were promising not to quit, because there was no way we could know with any certainty what the future would hold. The sturdiness of a marriage is affirmed not on the wedding day but ten or fifteen or twenty years later, when both partners are still striving (imperfectly!) to keep those vows. Waiting and testing and times of uncertainty are required for a promise to be realized as the beautiful thing that it is.

ॐ

You may or may not know this about me, but I play the upright bass. It's a stringed instrument—the largest and lowest pitched one in a modern-day symphony orchestra. The bass weighs between twenty and twenty-five pounds, and its case probably weighs about as much. I began playing it when I was ten. That year, a high school quintet came to perform for my fourth-grade music class to show us what the different instruments looked and sounded like. Naturally, I fell in love with the one that was almost as big as me.

Our teacher told us that we could choose any of the instruments we heard that day to learn to play. "Any of them?" I asked her, already knowing which one I had my eye on.

"Well, yes," she said, "except the bass. Because girls don't play bass."

I clearly remember thinking that was the most ridiculous thing I'd ever heard. I couldn't believe she was telling me I couldn't do something just because I was a *girl*. I must have gone home and explained to my parents that I simply had to play the bass, regardless of the girl-prohibition. Thankfully, they saw it from my point of view and agreed to let me try. They composed a note to the well-meaning music teacher and signed it, saying that in spite of the obvious fact of my gender, I did indeed have their permission to break the mold and learn to play the bass. (Score one for the girls!)

I took this rocky beginning with my new instrument as

a kind of personal challenge. I practiced hard and poured a lot of my time into learning. Because the bass is also a very expensive instrument, we rented one from a local music store in the beginning. But as time went on (and when they could see that this wasn't a passing fling), Mom and Dad promised that if I kept at it, they would get me my own bass. By the time I got to high school, I was a much better musician and getting more opportunities to play, so I needed a good-quality instrument. We heard from my teacher that a friend of a friend had discovered the body of an old bass in the storage attic of a music store . . . in Chicago. It had no neck, no fingerboard and no strings, but it had a rich history and "great bones."

"It's old," my teacher reported, "and was made in Germany. If someone could just restore this thing, I know it would sound *amazing*."

My parents bought that antique bass for me sight-unseen, had it shipped to South Carolina, and found a restorer willing to work on it. It took time. It literally had to be reassembled piece by piece. Today, that bass is one of my most valued possessions. I carried it all across the nation with me for years as I performed with artists like Steven Curtis Chapman, Mac Powell of Third Day, and even once with bluegrass songbird Alison Krauss. I played it during my college days with a band called Silers Bald, and I still play it today. I treasure it, not just for the miles we've traveled together but for its story. It was a gift remade—re-created, really—by a skilled craftsman who recognized its worth, and then it was placed in my care. The music that has come from it represents a host of people besides just me, and I am grateful for the preparation and providence that made me ready to receive it in God's time.

I don't know that "good things come to those who wait" just *because* they wait, but I know this much for sure: there is a blessing that comes from waiting on the Lord and an intimacy that comes from walking through uncertain times with him. We can't always see what is happening in the waiting, but we can be sure in the meantime that God's plan for us is good and his promises are true.

I said that God initiated one more covenant with his people after the covenant he made with King David, and this one was a long time coming. A thousand or so years and twenty-eight generations after David's death, a baby was born in the tiny town of Bethlehem of Judea. He was the fulfillment of every promise of God to man from Adam forward. Jesus Christ was born to Mary and Joseph (a descendant of David), but his true Father was God. In the words of the priest Zechariah:

> Blessed be the Lord God of Israel,
>   for he has visited and redeemed his people
> and has raised up a horn of salvation for us
>   in the house of his servant David,
> as he spoke by the mouth of his holy prophets from
>   of old,
> that we should be saved from our enemies
>   and from the hand of all who hate us;

> to show the mercy promised to our fathers
> and to remember his holy covenant,
> the oath that he swore to our father Abraham, to grant us
> that we, being delivered from the hand of our enemies,
> might serve him without fear,
> in holiness and righteousness before him all our
> days. (Luke 1:68–75 ESV)

This child, predicted Zechariah, would redeem his people, bringing salvation. This child would embody the mercy promised to the fathers of old. The birth of Jesus would usher in the new covenant, providing everything required by God to deliver his people from their greatest enemy, the deadly consequences of sin—permanently. In Jesus, Paul said, all the promises of God are "yes" and "amen" (see 2 Cor. 1:20).

What does that mean to you and me? To people living in the twenty-first century who don't happen to be Jewish? "If you are Christ's," wrote Paul, "then you are Abraham's offspring, heirs according to promise" (Gal. 3:29 ESV). The promises God made to Abraham are realized for you and me in Jesus. The Son of God is *our* redeemer. He is *our* inheritance. He is *our* king, *our* priest, *our* atoning sacrifice. All the promises of God to man from the beginning of time find their ultimate answer in him. Through Christ, we are made his people, and he declares himself forever our God!

Do you see the mighty faithfulness of God? Friend, every promise our Father makes, he keeps. We can trust him to hold on to us, even when we aren't holding on to him. In Jesus, who is the embodiment of every element of God's covenant with man, God provides the very holiness he requires! He doesn't just help us to be faithful in the moment—he attributes Jesus' perfect faithfulness to us once and for all! Our loving, promising God is both the covenant maker and the covenant keeper. And that is a very good thing indeed.

I was reminded of this covenant-keeping nature of God the first time Josie and I walked together on a beach. We were at Seabrook Island, near Kiawah Island, South Carolina. Most of our friends in Atlanta like to go to the Florida beaches, but Martin and I grew up visiting the beaches of South Carolina, and even today I'm more drawn to the marshes and wildlife there than I am to the crystal-blue waters of Florida, as perfect as they are.

Josie had just begun walking, and it was her first time exploring the shoreline on foot. At first it was frightening to her—the gulls, the noise, the pull of the surf—and she gripped my hand tightly. But it wasn't long before her fear gave way to curiosity, and while I was fully aware of the ocean's tides and undertows and scary creatures, she was not. Her grip on my hand loosened, but mine on hers never did. I didn't let her go when she stopped to examine a shell or point to a shore bird. I didn't let her go when she wanted to touch the wet sand with her hands. There was never a minute when her security was in question. Because this girl is mine and I love her with all my heart, I held on to her—even when she wasn't holding on to me. I always will.

Our promise-keeping God holds us fast. He will not let us go. His promises are for us, yes. But they don't depend on us. And his promises pursue us to the end.

Years ago, at a point in my life when not a lot was going

right, I wrote a song called "He Will Not Let Go." I felt as though I had hit rock bottom, as though God could never use me. I wondered if maybe I were damaged goods and would be sidelined forever, unqualified to serve him. But in spite of how I felt, I knew God's love for me was stronger than my emotions and that it held firm despite my actions. Maybe I wrote and sang this song more for myself than for anyone else, but I believe that God's mercy and goodness will follow me all the days of my life—and that it will follow you too:

It may take time, on this journey slow
What lies ahead, I'm not sure I know
But the hand that holds this flailing soul
He will not let go . . .
When all around my soul gives way
He then is all my hope and stay
When grief has paralyzed my heart
His grip holds even tighter than the dark
I've heard it said, this too shall pass
The joy will come, that the hurt won't last
So I will trust that within His grasp
I am not alone
For He will not let go.[1]

Our God is so good. He is trustworthy. He keeps his promises. He will not let you go.

WHITE FLAG PRAYER #6

You are a promise-keeping God. I surrender to
you and trust you to never let me go. Amen.

PART THREE

How Do I Surrender?

SEVEN

Surrender by Letting Go

I don't know about you, but I've got a good grip. I mean, I can hold on like nobody's business. I can hold on to old hurts, even when I know they're not doing me any good. I can hold on to faulty ideas, even after they've been proven wrong. I can hold on to pride by refusing to ask for help, believing that asking would be the same as admitting weakness. I can cling to the moral high ground in a situation where a little grace would be way more Christlike, not to mention constructive. And if I'm not careful, I can hold on so tightly to yesterday's blessings that I couldn't possibly receive anything new from God today.

After Ben and Griffin were born and our family expanded in a day from three humans to five, I was drowning. I mean *drowning*. We had three children under the age of two, Martin and I were struggling to establish our "new normal" in work and marriage and parenting roles, and I was receiving lots of invitations to sing and speak outside my regular job at Perimeter.

This was all good stuff, for sure, and I was grateful for every single bit of it, but it was a lot to manage all at once. Just keeping the babies fed some days seemed like an impossible challenge, nursing them both and supplementing my nursing with bottle feedings every two to three hours. (I'd barely finish one feeding before it was time to start again!) There didn't seem to be enough of me to go around most days, but I was determined not to let anyone down. We'd prayed for these children, after all—we believed they were a gift from God. For us, me not returning to work was not an option. And as much as I love my work, I love being a mom too. The balance is not an easy one.

When I look back on that time, I can see that my death grip on all of this was hurting us and was especially hurting me. Not only was I trying desperately to manage my new situation (even while feeling totally out of control), I was clinging to some pretty messed-up thinking as well. I had the idea that my competency as a mother depended on whether or not I could wrangle a toddler and two babies every day without a meltdown (theirs or mine). I had the idea that if I did not say yes to most of the ministry invitations that were coming my way, they'd simply stop coming. I may have even had the idea that to admit to anyone how frazzled and tired I was would be seen as being ungrateful for the three beautiful children God had given to Martin and me.

To say my head was not in a very good place would be an understatement. If I'd taken the time to really pray all this through, I might have recognized my faulty thinking, but I hardly had time for a quick shower, much less a half hour of extended prayer. "Help me, Lord!" was the extent of my not-so-quiet time most mornings, but even that hurried SOS was a prayer God in his mercy answered.

The twins were less than two weeks old when I received a call from a church friend about a young woman she knew. My friend explained that this girl was struggling with an eating disorder and in a very rough place emotionally. I felt my stomach begin to tighten. I thought I knew what was coming next and dreaded hearing the words "Would you be willing to meet with her? Could you possibly help her?" *Oh my gosh. Help her? Are you kidding? I can barely help myself.* I was already thinking of how to say a polite "not now" to her request, but coming to *her* aid wasn't exactly what God had in mind.

"She's not able to work full-time right now," my friend said, "but she needs something to do. She's got a ton of time on her hands, and her thoughts are eating her alive. I was wondering if maybe she might come and help you out with the babies. I know you're buried at home." *Oh. Well, yes. That would be fantastic, actually. And so not what I was thinking.*

This arrangement—as unconventional as it sounded— turned out to be an amazing gift to us both. I desperately needed the extra pair of hands—there was no arguing that! And my new young friend needed someone else to talk to and something positive to do with her time. For several weeks she came to our house and pitched in, doing whatever job needed to be done. She helped with the boys, helped with Josie, and blessed us every single day by her presence. She felt productive and valued and heard, and I felt rescued. I am in no way a professional counselor, and she was not a certified nanny. But we two amateurs each had something valuable to offer the other, and by letting go of our determination to help ourselves by ourselves, we were both able to receive what we needed most.

For a season (and a very precious one at that), I traded one-way ministry to thousands for mutual, one-to-one ministry with another human being who was just as needy as I was. My new friend traded a high-energy job for something more temporary, less visible, and much less glamorous. And we both learned it is impossible to accept anything from God when you're holding on tightly to something else, even if it's your own pride. Receiving one thing new always requires the letting go of something else.

The empty spaces in between where we are and what's next often terrify us, yet every single letting go requires moments of uncertainty where we seem suspended between what was and what isn't yet. During these times we don't feel like we're holding on to anything solid at all or being held by anyone.

Have you lived through one of these less-than-comfortable spaces? Maybe you're in one of them now. Maybe you're between forgiveness and reconciliation, not even sure that reconciliation is possible. Maybe you're between a promise and its anticipated fulfillment, or a grueling medical treatment and its hoped-for healing. Maybe you've found yourself between a hard question and its slow-to-arrive answer, or between a willing sacrifice and its so-very-worth-it reward. Let's be honest here. In-between is both a hard place to live and a necessary part of letting go. It's also the incredibly fertile place where our faith is strengthened and our understanding grows.

I don't know about you, but I rarely see the whole picture of what God's up to all at once or understand the significance of a hurt or a challenge while I'm in the middle of it. A lag almost always exists for me between surrender and security, between faith and sight. I can know in my head that placing my trust in God and giving over control to him is *right*, but that doesn't mean I feel terrific in the moment about letting go. And honestly, it's okay that I don't.

God's word is full of the testimonies of those who have struggled mightily with their in-between spaces on the journey from surrender to faith. I'm thinking now of Esther, who risked her life appearing before her husband, King Ahasuerus, to plead for justice for her Jewish kinsmen. She knew that she was breaking protocol by approaching the king without being called, and she knew that the confession of her Jewish heritage could mean rejection by him—or even banishment or death. But the survival of her people required her trust and her courage. Can you imagine how she must have felt in the moments between her request to Ahasuerus to save her people and the king's favorable response? She had no way of knowing what his answer would be. She only knew she had to ask.

Can you imagine how Hannah felt, pleading with God year after year in the temple for a child, taunted by her husband's *other* wife, Peninnah, who seemed to have sons and daughters to spare? Her pain and longing were so powerful that Eli the priest mistook her desperate prayers for drunkenness, and even her husband made light of her desire: "Hannah, why do you weep? And why do you not eat? And why is your heart sad? Am I not more to you than ten sons?" (1 Sam. 1:8 ESV). *Well, um, no, Elkanah, dear. Not exactly.*

Hannah publicly and persistently exposed her longing before God and others—and then she waited. "In due time," we're told, the Lord remembered her. She conceived and had a son named Samuel. But she lived for who-knows-how-long between her "great anxiety and vexation" and her "due time," trusting God the whole way. (Hannah really surrendered twice: she pledged this precious son to God for his use and his glory, and he became a great prophet. But that's another story.)

Or what about Joseph, trusting God for his future even while he was jailed in a foreign land for a crime he did not commit? Joseph's brothers had sold him into slavery in Egypt, but Joseph continued to believe God was with him, and God's care for him soon became evident to the Egyptian officer, Potiphar, too. At least it did until Potiphar's wife falsely accused Joseph of rape. Then this son of Israel was tossed into prison like a rapist and seemed to be forgotten for good—but not by God. God remembered Joseph, and eventually he gained a place of favor with Pharaoh—this time positioned to save and forgive the very brothers who betrayed him to begin with (see Genesis chapters 37, 39-45)! Joseph's story ended well, but it's no easy thing to keep on trusting God's timing when you see no immediate change in your situation.

Even Jesus experienced that terrible in-between space as he pleaded with God in prayer the night of his arrest. He knew the plan of God, but he was soul-sick over what lay in store. All alone and "greatly distressed and troubled," he cried out to God: "Abba, Father, all things are possible for you. Remove this cup from me. Yet not what I will, but what you will" (Mark 14:36 ESV). As a Son, Jesus told his Father how he longed for things to be. Then he submitted that desire to the will of the Father and steadfastly, whole-heartedly embraced the cross. The apostle Peter described Jesus' surrender like this: "He committed no sin, neither was deceit found in his mouth. When he was reviled, he did not revile in return; when he suffered, he did not threaten, but continued entrusting himself to him who judges justly" (1 Peter 2:22–23 ESV).

Jesus had all the power of God in him. He could have changed his situation in an instant, yet he surrendered his will to the Father, just like you and I are called to do.

Of all the in-between times recorded in Scripture, this one encourages me the most: Jesus' time in the tomb between his death and his resurrection. Can you imagine a darker time? A more hopeless and heartbreaking time? His disciples had seen their beloved rabbi murdered, betrayed by one of their own, tried by their religious leaders, and sentenced to death by a weak-willed but politically savvy Roman bureaucrat. The hopes of Jesus' followers for a national deliverer had been dashed to pieces, and his mother had watched her precious, God-promised son die a terrible, painful, undeserved death.

"The crucifixion of Jesus," says theologian N. T. Wright,

"was the symbol not merely of hope deferred *but of hope crushed and trampled upon*" (emphasis mine).[1] If ever there was a place of awful, terrible waiting, it was the burial place of Jesus. On Friday evening his body was placed in a borrowed grave. Saturday his burial place was guarded by Roman soldiers. No one came, and nothing changed. Silence. Until Sunday. But that Sunday changed everything. *Everything.*

On that morning, Jesus' mother and other women who followed Jesus came to the tomb to prepare Jesus' body for a more permanent burial. (There had been no time for this when Jesus was removed from the cross on Friday. The Jewish Sabbath was fast approaching, and his friends were only able to arrange for a temporary burial place—nothing more.) But the huge stone that had been placed across the opening of his grave—the one they were discussing how to move—was already rolled away. The grave was open. And Jesus was not there. A being dressed in dazzling white reported stunning news: "Do not be alarmed. You seek Jesus of Nazareth, who was crucified. He has risen; he is not here. See the place where they laid him. But go, tell his disciples and Peter that he is going before you to Galilee. There you will see him, just as he told you" (Mark 16:6–7 ESV).

The fact of the resurrection gives me real hope in the space between surrender and Sunday. I can trust the God who defeated sin and death for me for good. My Jesus surrendered once for all, for all of us. Thank goodness you and I are only called to imitate him in surrender little by little, one moment at a time.

$\backsim$

I remember a hymn from childhood called "I Surrender All." It's an old song, written by a lay Methodist preacher named J. W. Van DeVenter in the late 1800s. Each one of the hymn's five stanzas begins with the words "all to Jesus I surrender," and the chorus contains the phrase "I surrender all" three times, plus two more in the men's part. Anyone who sings the entire hymn would sing the word *surrender* thirty times and the word *all* forty-three times! That's a lot of surrendering it all, friend.

That same hymn has been sung over and over in the more than one hundred years since it was written. It's been recorded countless times, too, in hymn collections by dozens of artists in genres from rap to hip hop to pop to Southern gospel. My point is this: surrender is an ongoing process. None of us surrenders just once—or ever quite surrenders *all*. On this side of eternity, we will never be done with surrender. It's not a one-time decision for us. It's a commitment to a *lifestyle*. Every day will bring us a new opportunity to offer our surrender to God, to let something go. And we'll keep on giving over to God things we thought we released to him fully once and for all but didn't. Not because we didn't want to—because we couldn't yet.

Martin and I are sometimes asked if we still pray for God to heal him from the effects of his brain tumor and surgeries. The answer is yes, we both do. But I think the more important question (and hardly anyone asks *this*) is whether we still surrender to God's plan for our lives *with* the lingering effects of his illness. Do we surrender to the daily challenges of only one of us driving? (We do.) Do we surrender to receiving the help we need from time to time to make our crazy schedules work? (We do.) Do we surrender to a redefining of the roles we both anticipated when we married? (We do.) Do we surrender to me reminding Martin—and to him being reminded of, daily—the things most couples remember to do without thinking? (We do.) We don't always do it gracefully, but we do it often.

We made promises to each other in our wedding vows. They were bold words. They may seem ordinary because almost everyone says them, but they're not. Not at all. We said words like "for better, for worse" and "for richer, for poorer" and "in sickness and in health." And there was no expiration date mentioned; just the opposite. We promised for "as long as we both shall live." We didn't know that day what the future would bring. We had no way of knowing that in a very short time, we would be called upon to make good on some of those big promises.

Neither of us would have chosen these challenges to be a part of our life together. But in God's providence, they are. Our challenges may be different from yours, but they are no more or less difficult than those others face. They are just *ours*. And we have to keep on saying yes to this precious and imperfect life God has given us, surrendering to him the things we might still wish to change about it. *Just like everyone else we know.*

If I were in control of my life, sitting on the "throne," I might decree that no uncertainty, suffering, broken relationships, or conflict would exist. Maybe I'd issue a "royal order" to put an end to all pain and heartbreak, because really— who needs that stuff? I might even do away with waiting and struggle and confusion while I was at it. But if I did this—if

I had my way—I wouldn't make the world a better place or make myself a better person. How do I know? Because the things I'd eliminate are the very things God uses to draw me closer to him in trust and dependence and to make me more like his beautiful Son. The things I'd do away with are the things he does good with!

Because of the sacrificial death and resurrection of Jesus, we have peace with God—even in the midst of suffering or doubt or trouble. Because of him, we are becoming people who are able to "boast in the hope of the glory of God" (Rom. 5:2 NIV). We don't just praise God for what he's going to do for us "by and by" and slog through the trials of this life with grim determination. (How awful would that be?) Instead:

> We also glory in our sufferings, because we know that suffering produces perseverance; perseverance, character; and character, hope. And hope does not put us to shame, because God's love has been poured out into our hearts through the Holy Spirit, who has been given to us. (Rom. 5:3–5 NIV)

No matter what I face, I have good reason to hope, every single day. And no matter what happens in my life, God's love never stops being poured out into my heart. That gift is an endless resource—not by and by but here and now.

♄

I'm a worshiper of God first and foremost, but I'm also a worship leader by vocation. Worship leaders have a unique perspective in corporate worship: we don't see ourselves; we see you. We see God's people offering to him their worship, hundreds, sometimes thousands of you at a time. From that perspective, I can tell you something with 100 percent certainty: I've never seen anyone worship with clenched fists. It just doesn't happen. No one raises their fists to God to offer him praise and honor and glory.

What I do see, and often, is a sea of open hands raised toward heaven. Arms up. Palms out. Fingers extended. Holding on to nothing. My prayer for myself—and for you—is that we would peel our fingers back from whatever it is we're clutching and release it to God. Even if it's our own brokenness. May the posture of our hearts be surrender to the one who is wise and strong and powerful and good and who loves us beyond reason. This is our choice—and our true worship.

WHITE FLAG PRAYER #7

God, I confess my need to gain and keep control of things and ask for your help in letting go of _____. It's all yours. Now help me leave it there with you. Amen.

EIGHT

Surrender by Choosing to Believe

Someone has said that the great issue of faith is not whether we believe in God but whether we believe the God we believe *in*. I think that must have been what the father who sought healing for his boy meant when he said to Jesus, "I do believe; help me overcome my unbelief!" (Mark 9:24 NIV). In other words, "Jesus, I believe in you as a healer, that you have power over disease—but I'm having some doubts in this moment that you are going to heal my son." In order to surrender his son's illness to Jesus, this good father had to choose belief: not just that Jesus *could* heal his son but that Jesus *would*.

Every surrender to God involves choosing to believe him.

When we surrender control of our lives to him, we're choosing belief over doubt, choosing belief over fear, choosing belief over worry and confusion and hopelessness. We're affirming the sovereignty of the God we say we believe in, at this present moment, in this particular circumstance.

Every moment of this life is not storybook perfect. Every day is not Leo and Kate on the bow of the *Titanic*, leaning into the wind and crowing, "King of the world!" (In fact, very few of *my* days feel that boldly triumphant!) Just like the man with the ailing son, most of us need help believing the God we believe in. We need help taking every thought captive and trusting God's Word over our own feelings.

When the crowds that followed Jesus asked him, "What must we do, to be doing the works of God?" he told them, "This is the work of God, that you believe in him whom he has sent" (John 6:28–29 ESV). In other words, Jesus said, "Believe in *me*. That's your assignment. That's the work you absolutely *must* do."

Thankfully, we don't have to summon our belief in Jesus out of thin air. We have help. God the Holy Spirit helps us to believe. The Scriptures help us to believe. Worship and liturgy encourage our belief, and so do those believers—saints past and present—who share our faith. We've already talked about the importance of trusting Scripture beyond our feelings when the two don't match. One particular psalm of David, Psalm 19, helps me to understand the benefit of this by stating a truth about God's Word, then responding with the positive result of that same truth:

> The law of the LORD is perfect,
>   refreshing the soul.
> The statutes of the LORD are trustworthy,
>   making wise the simple.
> The precepts of the LORD are right,
>   giving joy to the heart.

The commands of the LORD are radiant,
giving light to the eyes. (Ps. 19:7–8 NIV)

God's perfect law, said David, helps me by restoring or refreshing my soul. The word for *perfect* translates to "whole or complete." In other words, God's law covers every aspect of my life. There's nothing I can encounter in my spiritual life that the totality of God's Word does not address. The laws of men and their reasoning may prove incomplete or imperfect, but God's laws are wholly sufficient for my needs. My soul is refreshed by studying, believing, and obeying them.

Worldly wisdom can sometimes appear like the blind leading the blind. One "expert" can advise one thing, while a different "expert" advises another. God's commands are not like that. They're not confusing or puzzling, not given to trip us up or catch us in a mistake. Trying to follow his instruction is not like fumbling for my keys in the dark. Knowing his commands and obeying them is illuminating, and having that single, solid source of truth is like being lit from within.

Other Christians encourage us to believe and keep on believing God too. Worshiping together with God's family helps to strengthen our belief as we follow the familiar order of service or liturgy in praise, prayer, and personal repentance. "Every service is a structure of acts and words," C. S. Lewis once said, "[that] enables us to do these things best—if you like, it 'works' best—when, through long familiarity, we don't have to think about it. . . . The perfect church service would be one we were almost unaware of; our attention would have been on God."[1]

One of the things our senior pastor at Perimeter has

encouraged our worship team to do is create service beginnings that reflect a more reverent and awe-inspired approach to the Holy God we come together to worship. We strive to always begin with who God is and what he has done, not who we are or what we are doing. We try to orient ourselves and the congregation with the global, historical, cosmic story of God, looking beyond his engagement in our personal stories. And we begin worship focused on God's transcendence, rather than his imminence, because his nearness can only be appreciated and rightly welcomed when we begin to comprehend his complete other-ness.

Rightly ordered worship invites our right response to God and presents a compelling reason to give him the honor and glory he deserves. We believe that by beginning with God and not ourselves, our services will have a domino effect of worship in every aspect of life.

I know people who argue that we can worship God alone just as well as we can worship him together. But sometimes my own faith is weak, and corporate worship allows me to let others believe on my behalf until my heart can catch up. When I'm focused on God—who he is and what he's done— I'm less likely to get stuck on how I feel. And when I'm doing that together with his people, people whose struggles and victories I know, my belief is strengthened, and my momentary unbelief is more easily overcome.

I've always been drawn to the story in the Gospels of the bleeding woman. (Honestly, I feel bad that she's not named and is only known by her disease. Should we call her Jane? Mary?) Her boldness to take action based on her belief inspires me in a big way. She had a once-in-a-lifetime opportunity, and she went for it. Do you remember her story?

This woman suffered from a disease that caused her to hemorrhage nonstop for twelve years. She quietly joined the crowd that pressed around Jesus one day as he traveled through Caesarea Philippi—all of the people wanting his attention, his touch, his healing. Because of her bleeding, she was regarded as "unclean," with no standing at all, no recourse. Doctors had treated her for years, the Gospels tell us, but with no success.

Can you imagine how desperate she must have been? Her ritual uncleanness (and her modesty about it) made putting herself before Jesus and asking directly for healing impossible. She had spent all her savings seeking health. She was never welcome in the temple. Not being able to join her family and friends in worship made her lonely and a social outcast. But she imagined on that day if she could just approach Jesus unnoticed and touch even the edge of his robe, her small act of faith might invite his mercy and healing power. She had one instant, one available moment to act on her belief, and she seized it:

> She came up behind him and touched the fringe of his garment, and immediately her discharge of blood ceased. And Jesus said, "Who was it that touched me?" When all denied it, Peter said, "Master, the crowds surround you and are pressing in on you!" But Jesus said, "Someone touched me, for I perceive that power has gone out from

me." And when the woman saw that she was not hidden, she came trembling, and falling down before him declared in the presence of all the people why she had touched him, and how she had been immediately healed. And he said to her, "Daughter, your faith has made you well; go in peace." (Luke 8:44–48 ESV)

We won't ever experience the rewards of belief without the risk of belief. Acting on our belief in God in the present moment is risky. It requires courage and faith. But when we do it, we have a story to tell that echoes God's greater story—the story of a God who rescues, redeems, helps, heals, and restores those who place their faith in him. It's not enough for you and me to talk about belief, write about belief, or plan to act on our belief someday. We must grab opportunities when we see them, surrendering our fear to his certain providence and love.

Not only do we choose belief in the present moment, but God's children are also called to choose belief in the "messy middle" of things, including our suffering and grief. Choosing to believe God when a situation remains unresolved, a prayer is not answered as we hoped, or sorrow is bearing down on us is a serious lesson in surrender. It's not kids' stuff. It's not for sissies.

Let's face it: not everything gets fixed in this life in the way we wish it would. Not every prayer we pray receives the answer we long for, when we long for it. I never wanted my husband to become sick or struggle with disability. I never wanted to experience the gut-wrenching pain of infertility or the failed adoption or miscarriage that was to come or for our youngest son to be born needing surgery before he was a few months old. In every single case, I have prayed for 100 percent health and wholeness for those I love. But God has had a different plan. And although his plan for us is perfect, every aspect of our lives is not.

I've always been struck by the story of Job—by the fact that, while you and I are told the "why" behind Job's devastation, Job never knew this side of heaven. We read in the Bible that God allowed Satan to strike Job with trouble, within limits. But Job wasn't privy to that conversation when it happened, and no one reported it to him. He just lived in the very messy middle of the fallout of Satan's relentless jabs. He endured natural disasters, financial ruin, the death of loved ones, and the deterioration of his own health without a single word of explanation. And somehow, he kept on believing the God he believed in.

Things got so bad for Job that his wife encouraged him to curse God and die—just to get all that suffering over with. Job refused. "Shall we receive good from God," he asked her, "and shall we not receive evil?" (Job 2:10 ESV).

Job's three friends—Eliphaz, Bildad, and Zophar—weren't helpful either. Oh, at first they sat quietly and grieved with him, a good response when a friend suffers. But before long they were offering their own half-baked explanations for Job's sad predicament. Eliphaz said he'd never seen the innocent perish or the upright cut off, implying that perhaps Job was neither innocent nor upright. "Can mortal man be in the right before God?" he wanted to know. "Can a man be pure before his Maker?" (Job 4:17 ESV). He urged Job to seek God and continue to "commit [his] cause" to him (Job 5:8 ESV), and he predicted that God would eventually deliver Job from his troubles and redeem him. But he offered next to nothing to comfort Job in the middle of his crisis. Just a lot of moralizing.

Bildad urged Job to repent—for himself and on behalf of his children—and plead to God for mercy. He told Job that God would not reject a blameless man, but Job responded that no man is blameless before God, not even a man with a reputation as fine as Job's. Bildad assumed that a direct connection existed between some past sin of Job's and the present pain he was enduring. And in the meantime, Job continued to feel the full weight of his suffering:

> For he crushes me with a tempest
>   and multiplies my wounds without cause;
> he will not let me get my breath,
>   but fills me with bitterness.
> If it is a contest of strength, behold, he is mighty!
>   If it is a matter of justice, who can summon him?
>   (Job 9:17–19 ESV)

Eliphaz and Bildad were bad enough, but Job's buddy Zophar may win the prize for least helpful friend: he basically told Job that while his situation was bad, he really deserved worse!

> For you say, "My doctrine is pure,
>   and I am clean in God's eyes,"

But oh, that God would speak
and open his lips to you,
and that he would tell you the secrets of wisdom!
For he is manifold in understanding.
Know then that God exacts of you less than your guilt
deserves. (Job 11:4–6 ESV)

Wow! *So* not encouraging.

After hearing his friends out, Job came to a powerful conclusion. Clearly, no easy answers exist for his messy middle. His friends were blowing hot air, and his God was strangely silent. Meanwhile, Job's suffering dragged on. Have you been there, friend? I sure have. Every single one of us has moments when all we know is that we hurt, and nothing anyone says can change that. There are times when we long to see his handwriting in the sky or hear an audible explanation for our suffering, but we are met with only silence. Crickets.

Job insisted that he wanted an audience with God to plead his case, and he desired relief from his suffering. But he asserted in the big, bad middle of his pain, "Though he slay me, I will hope in him" (Job 13:15 ESV). He chose to believe God in the very place he was hurting.

When our girl was almost one I became pregnant again, but this time I experienced a miscarriage—an early one, at seven or eight weeks. I was touring with friends Steven Curtis Chapman and Jason Gray, and I had told the band

I was expecting only a few days before. We had just rolled into Indiana and had a show to do that night.

An hour or so before show time I noticed some bleeding. *Is this . . . oh please no. Could it be—is this a miscarriage?*

Sitting alone with Josie in my tiny dressing room, I felt completely lost about what to do next. Martin was more than five hundred miles and three states away in Atlanta. The audience had already begun to file into the venue. As the minutes ticked down, I finally told Steven and Jason what I feared. The words were barely out of my mouth before they began to pray with me. And I don't mean they huddled up and said a quick, "God bless Laura." They laid hands on me and pled with the Father on my behalf with all the empathy and compassion of two brothers in Christ who are loving dads to their own precious children.

They both insisted that I didn't have to sing that night—but singing or not singing wouldn't have changed what was happening one bit. So I did my set, including the song "God of Every Story." Somehow, I made it all the way through, including the chorus:

> He's the God of every story . . .
> He sees each tear that falls . . .
> We may not understand, but one thing is certain . . .
> He's a faithful, faithful God.[2]

I held it together (barely), but behind me the band was weeping. These consummate Nashville musicians were crying their eyes out, and the audience had no idea why. Later that night on the bus, what I feared was happening finally did. I texted back and forth with Martin at 3:00 a.m. and tried not to cry out loud and wake up the others. But strangely, even though my precious husband wasn't nearly close enough and everyone else around me was asleep, I felt cared for. Safe. I chose to believe God that night. That he *is* the God of every story, including mine. And that somehow, he would make a way for us to have the family that we'd dreamed of.

Let me say this to my sisters who've experienced what I did: just because miscarriages happen frequently, that doesn't make them ordinary. The loss of a baby before it is born is still a death. It's still a grief. The clinical explanation that "the fetus was not viable" doesn't cover the half of it. That sterile terminology may be true, but it makes the very real loss of life sound like a science experiment gone wrong instead of the loss of an already-loved baby boy or girl who never experienced life outside the womb.

I confess I'm not so good at grief. I graduated from the school of "Suck it up, buttercup" with a major in "Put your big girl pants on and deal with it." My children are shocked when they see me cry ("Mommy, what's that stuff coming out of your eye?"), and sometimes I'm surprised too. Grief doesn't always look productive to me. It feels more like a black hole that, if I let myself sink into, I might not crawl out of alive. If I give in to the hurt, will a twenty-minute ugly cry be enough to relieve the ache, or will this thing pummel me to pieces? Because, at the end of the day, there's still carpool to drive, right?

I may be a theologian with the degree to prove it, but I still have no go-to formula for how best to process grief. Maybe there is no "best" way. I'm pretty sure of one thing, though: any time we experience pain, grief is a wholly appropriate response. Tears are appropriate for the grieving. Weeping with those who weep is right and good, both for the comforted and for the comforter. And choosing to believe God in the middle of our grief is a powerful, powerful decision indeed. I agree with the wise person who observed, "We should never be afraid to trust an unknown future to a known God." (Or to cry while we're doing it.)

We're called to believe God in the messy middle of our story, when sorrow and grief threaten to railroad belief. We are also called to believe God for the long view, for the ending we can't yet see.

When we surrender to his plan for our lives, we surrender to the entire scope of it, beginning to end, A to Z—not just the parts we like. The entire scope remains mostly invisible to us. God does not reveal all his ways in advance or answer our every "why?" when asked. We may get stuck in the moment, especially when the moment threatens or challenges us. But our God is the God of yesterday, today, and forever. He's got the whole thing covered, start to glorious finish.

Sometimes when I need a pep talk for believing to the end, I read Hebrews 11 and 12. (I highly recommend both chapters.) Chapter 12 begins with this strong encouragement:

> Therefore, since we are surrounded by such a great cloud
> of witnesses, let us throw off everything that hinders
> and the sin that so easily entangles. And let us run with

perseverance the race marked out for us, fixing our eyes on Jesus, the pioneer and perfecter of faith. For the joy set before him he endured the cross, scorning its shame, and sat down at the right hand of the throne of God. Consider him who endured such opposition from sinners, so that you will not grow weary and lose heart. (vv. 1–3 NIV)

We sometimes think if a thing doesn't happen in our lifetime, it doesn't happen. (Or if it doesn't happen in a week, it doesn't happen!) God sees the long view, and on our journeys of belief we have the encouragement of "a great cloud of witnesses" who are always pointing us to Jesus. As they cheer for him, it encourages me! I cling to the stories of those believing witnesses who've gone before me, and I take plenty of encouragement from their lives. Our struggles aren't new. But in every age they testify to us that God is faithful to the end.

Hebrews 11 calls out many in the biblical "cloud of witnesses" who lived by faith, responded to God in faith, pressed on in faith, and received their due reward. Abel, Enoch, Noah, Abraham, Sarah, Moses, Gideon, David, and Samuel are named—and their historic victories are duly recorded. But the writer of Hebrews doesn't neglect other nameless saints whose stories didn't end in earthly glory. Midway through the thirty-fifth verse of the chapter, we read of these witnesses:

Some were tortured, refusing to accept release, so that they might rise again to a better life. Others suffered mocking and flogging, and even chains and imprisonment. They were stoned, they were sawn in two, they were killed with the sword. They went about in skins of sheep and goats,

destitute, afflicted, mistreated—of whom the world was
not worthy—wandering about in deserts and mountains,
and in dens and caves of the earth. (Heb. 11:35–38 ESV)

These, we're told, did not receive all the promises of God
in this life, "since God had provided something better for us"
(v. 40 ESV). These took the long view and believed their God
to the end, without immediate reward. They embraced the
certain hope of "a kingdom that cannot be shaken" (Heb.
12:28). And even though I'd prefer to be listed among the
named victorious, I'm just as encouraged by the unnamed
martyrs who suffered for their faith in this life. They judged
God faithful, and they kept on believing for what Paul called
"the guarantee of our inheritance until we acquire posses-
sion of it, to the praise of his glory" (Eph. 1:14 ESV).

In the present moment, in the long middle and to the
very end, nothing is better for us than to choose to believe
the great God we believe in.

Let me offer one more reason to choose belief: because of
the company we keep. We are God's beloved children. We
are co-heirs with Christ, our redeemer. We are filled by the
Holy Spirit, the pledge of our future inheritance of God's
kingdom. Why would we be afraid to surrender to the God
who gives us all this? Why wouldn't we believe him in the
here and now? When you're with the one you trust, why
wouldn't you be confident that all will end well?

Several years back, Martin and I were invited to speak

at a conference in Denmark. Denmark! Neither of us had been before, so we decided to arrive a few days early. We researched the area we'd be visiting and probably even googled "What to do in Denmark?" like the American tourists we were. One sight that captured our attention was the Møns Klint, a Danish nature reserve on the Baltic Sea. From what we read, it sounded fantastic: steep woodland trails, solid white, 120-meter chalk and limestone cliffs, and breathtaking sea views. Count us in!

When we got to the Cliffs of Moen, however, they were covered in ice. (To be fair, it *was* March.) There were plenty of signs, of course, but we couldn't read them. They were in Danish! So we struck out on a hiking trail, found the cliffs (they were fantastic!), and promptly lost our way when it began to snow. We were confused about which of the three different parking areas we'd started out from and wandered until it was almost dark. And we didn't pass another living soul.

Finally, we found our way back to where we'd started and returned after dark to our local B&B, laughing as we told our hosts where we'd been and what we'd done. Except they were horrified. They acted like we'd attempted to climb the infamous Cliffs of Insanity from *The Princess Bride*. They quickly explained that the park does not officially open until summer, and the trails were very treacherous in March, especially at the higher altitudes. And those beautiful, chalky cliffs? Huge pieces of them have a tendency to slip right into the Baltic Sea when wet! They could not believe what we'd done; they must have thought we were very careless.

The truth is, we probably were. We should have realized the risk. But we were also young and in love and willing to go anywhere together. I trusted Martin completely, and it never entered my mind to be afraid with him by my side. I was certain that, with him, nothing bad could possibly happen. We'd already had so many adventures together—and we'd survived them all! What was a little trek through the Cliffs of Moen?

Friend, with God by my side, I have no reason not to trust. My gaze should be so focused on him—I should be so enamored of who he is—that no perilous cliff could shake my belief. He and I have traveled the years together, and he's always been faithful. I won't lie: some trails have been hard. I've lost my way more than a time or two. But my safety and security—and my choice to believe—has its roots in the company I keep.

I can trust him. I do. But "oh, for grace to trust him more!"

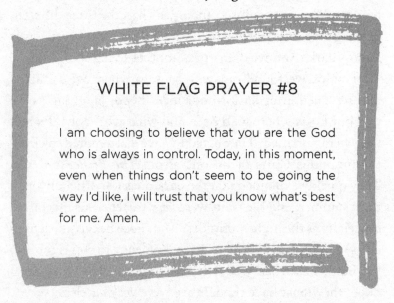

WHITE FLAG PRAYER #8

I am choosing to believe that you are the God who is always in control. Today, in this moment, even when things don't seem to be going the way I'd like, I will trust that you know what's best for me. Amen.

NINE

Surrender by Acting "As If"

*H*ave you ever been surprised to learn that someone is a Christian? (Or maybe wondered if you've surprised anyone else when they've learned of *your* faith?) Usually it's because they—or we—are not "acting the part," right? Maybe we're found in a place where someone who follows Christ wouldn't be expected to show up or we've behaved in a way they wouldn't be expected to behave. When circumstances and professed belief just don't line up, we tend to question the belief, not the circumstances.

I performed with a band called Silers Bald during my college years. Most of us who were with the band in those days worked other jobs. We had to. We were just beginning to catch on around the regional music circuit—playing a lot of campus shows and traveling from place to place on weekends. But because we weren't making any real money at music yet, we all had to do something else too. My "something else" for a while was working as the breadstick girl at the fast-casual Italian restaurant Fazoli's. (Breadsticks there were all-you-can-eat, so I earned my paycheck!)

One night at work I was taking an order from a really cute college guy and girl. I noticed the guy had on a Silers Bald T-shirt! How crazy is that? Trying to be as chill as possible, I gestured at his shirt: "So are you a fan of that band, Silers Bald?"

He said he was!

I hesitated for a second or two about whether or not to "out" myself and decided (against my better judgment) to go for it. After all, he'd already said he was a fan.

"Well, I'm a member of the band," I told him. "I play string bass with Silers Bald."

"You play bass in Silers Bald?" he asked.

"Yep." Okay. Let the gushing begin.

He eyed my shiny black polyester pants, my bright-red polyester shirt, and my very (at the time) un-hip, straight-billed Fazoli's cap. "Huh. I just saw them play at USC Downtown. But I don't remember seeing you, or any girl bass player."

Well he had me there. I hadn't played *that* particular show. I'd had a scheduling conflict, and it was one of the few gigs I missed in all my time with the band. I just sort of shrugged and felt like a total idiot because, at that point, who'd believe the uncool breadstick girl at Fazoli's was also the bass player for Silers Bald? I swear that couple avoided me for the rest of the night. They didn't ask me for any extra breadsticks, either, because let's face it—my story was less than believable. I didn't exactly look as if I was in a band of any kind!

My food server's position and my uniform screamed the exact opposite of what I claimed to be: a working musician. Trying to explain why I was pushing breadsticks at a local restaurant hardly seemed worth the effort since almost everything this couple had just observed contradicted the identity I'd claimed.

When I find myself feeling unsure of my identity in God's eyes, his Word offers me plenty of assurance about who I am in Christ. Ephesians 2, especially, gives me this helpful and hopeful reminder:

> But because of his great love for us, God, who is rich in mercy, made us alive with Christ even when we were dead in transgressions—it is by grace you have been saved. And God raised us up with Christ and seated us with him in the heavenly realms in Christ Jesus, in order that in the coming ages he might show the incomparable riches of his grace, expressed in his kindness to us in Christ Jesus. For it is by grace you have been saved, through faith—and this is not from yourselves, it is the gift of God—not by works, so that no one can boast. For we are God's handiwork, created in Christ Jesus to do good works, which God prepared in advance for us to do. (vv. 4–10 NIV)

This is who I am, and I still need to be reminded of it. If I believe what God says about me is true, I should be willing to double down on my belief at every opportunity. That means in times of discouragement or doubt or testing—or in times of joy or blessing or peace—I will choose to surrender to God by acting as if I am who he says I am, regardless of my circumstances.

My most recent success or my most recent failure does not define me any more than yours defines you. The world may say so, but that's not what God says. When I disappoint someone I love (and I do), *I* am not a disappointment. I am still a woman who is completely loved by God. He shows mercy to me whether I succeed or fail, whether I disappoint or please. When I sin (and I do) I am not defined by my sin, doomed to repeat my worst mistakes again and again. I am a beloved child of God who sinned, who can confess her sin and be forgiven, and who has the power *not* to sin again through the Holy Spirit who lives in me.

Each time I act as if what God says about me is true, I trust and honor him and defy the Devil. In every circumstance of my life, I can choose to take him at his word. But again, the choice is mine to make.

You know what I love about God's Word? Not only does it give me deep doctrinal passages like Ephesians 2 to help me understand my true identity, but it also gives me stories that let me see his divine principles at work in real people's lives! Better yet, most of those people seem a lot like me: their lives are messy, their hearts are not always strong, and their actions reveal some very human flaws.

Remember David? Ruth's great-grandson? The shepherd

boy who became Israel's second king? I like his story a *lot*. He was an underdog (nobody picked him to defeat the giant Goliath), a singer-songwriter (check out the Psalms), a bit of a late bloomer as far as careers go (he was Saul's "understudy" for what must have seemed like *forever*), and a guy with a few skeletons in his closet to say the least (see, oh, Bathsheba and Uriah, for starters).

We hear both about David and from David in Scripture. Books like 1 and 2 Samuel, 1 and 2 Kings, and 1 and 2 Chronicles report the facts of his life: son of Jesse, runt of a litter of boys, dreamer, musician, shepherd. Selected by the prophet Samuel to become king of Israel long before the current king, Saul, agreed his time was up. Killer of giants, leader of men, warrior, adulterer, murderer. Yep. You read that last bit right. And through it all, a man after God's own heart. How do we know that, based on the facts? Because we also have the Psalms.

Some of the psalms were written for gathered worship. Others read like a private, spiritual journal. In psalm after psalm, David pours out his heart before God. He praises. Confesses. Laments. Pleads. Rejoices. Promises. He holds nothing back! And why would he, anyway? He's certain God already knows him through and through (Psalm 139). Two particular stories about David (and the psalms corresponding to them) tell me that even in his worst moments, David acted as if he believed and trusted God. As if what God said—and not what David saw and felt—were true.

It's important to understand that David's life was deeply intertwined with Saul's. David served King Saul, playing music for him when the king was tormented and could not sleep. He befriended Saul's son Jonathan; the two men were like brothers. He was married to Saul's daughter Michal. But Saul did not accept the news that God had appointed David to become king in his place. Instead, he hunted David like a dog and tried to kill him rather than give up the throne of Israel before he was ready.

David fled Saul's court when he could no longer stay there safely. He didn't confront Saul and insist on a show-down, claiming that God had made him king. He ran. He hid among enemies. He hid in valleys and caves. And as he ran he gathered around him an army of misfits: disenfranchised men who were "in distress . . . in debt . . . and bitter in soul" (1 Sam. 22:2 ESV). They must have seen something in David they could relate to!

Two times while he was on the run, David had the chance to kill Saul and be done with the exhausting cat-and-mouse game the king was playing with him. Both times he refused. Would Saul have passed on an opportunity to murder David? Most surely not. But David believed he was who God said he was and that God would do what he said he would do. Saul only believed in Saul.

If there's anything more exhausting than running from your enemies, it must be running from your true identity in God. If there's anything more dangerous than waiting on God, it must be refusing to wait and taking your future into your own hands.

Imagine you are on the run from the person trying to take your life. You know he's on a rampage, and he's looking for you. You are hiding out deep in a cave, hoping not to be found, when your rival wanders into the mouth of that same cave for a restroom break. Your men urge you to take him by surprise and kill him, and you could. What do you do?

David did nothing but creep up behind Saul and cut off a small piece of his garment.

Why? As proof that he meant his king no harm. As evidence that he would not seize for himself what God promised but wait for it instead.

When Saul was again a safe distance away, David held up the proof of his refused opportunity and called out to him:

> "Why do you listen to the words of men who say, 'Behold, David seeks your harm'? Behold, this day your eyes have seen how the LORD gave you today into my hand in the cave. And some told me to kill you, but I spared you. I said, 'I will not put out my hand against my lord, for he is the LORD's anointed.' See, my father, see the corner of your robe in my hand. For by the fact that I cut off the corner of your robe and did not kill you, you may know and see that there is no wrong or treason in my hands. I have not sinned against you, though you hunt my life to take it." (1 Sam. 24:9–11 ESV)

David didn't need to kill Saul. Why not? Because he trusted God to work out God's plan on his behalf. To make good on his promises. He believed the same God who chose him to be king would set him on Israel's throne in his perfect time:

> "May the LORD judge between me and you, may the LORD avenge me against you, but my hand shall not be

against you. . . . After whom has the king of Israel come out? After whom do you pursue? After a dead dog! After a flea! May the LORD therefore be judge and give sentence between me and you, and see to it and plead my cause and deliver me from your hand." (vv. 12–15 ESV)

David's second opportunity to take things in his own hands happened very much like the first. Once again, he found himself in the presence of a vulnerable Saul—this time sleeping, with his spear near his head. Again, David's men urged him to do the deed; one even offered to kill Saul himself, saying it would only take one blow! David passed on this moment, too, but took Saul's spear and water jar to prove how near he'd been. From a distant hill he called out to Saul. Saul apologized for hunting David and begged him to come back. David wisely refused but offered to return Saul's gear to him if Saul would send a messenger for it. Then he told Saul the reason he did not take his life:

"The LORD rewards every man for his righteousness and his faithfulness, for the LORD gave you into my hand today, and I would not put out my hand against the LORD's anointed. Behold, as your life was precious this day in my sight, so may my life be precious in the sight of the LORD, and may he deliver me out of all tribulation." (1 Sam. 26:23–24 ESV)

David didn't act like someone who felt entitled to be king. He didn't act like someone who'd been terribly wronged by a leader he'd served loyally. He didn't trust Saul;

he trusted God. He acted as if he knew God had his back and would raise him up as he promised. And in time, God did. Meanwhile, David followed his own advice, recorded in Psalm 37:

> Commit your way to the LORD;
>> trust in him, and he will act.
> He will bring forth your righteousness as the light,
>> and your justice as the noonday.
> Be still before the LORD and wait patiently for him;
>> fret not yourself over the one who prospers in
>>> his way,
>> over the man who carries out evil devices!
> Refrain from anger, and forsake wrath!
>> Fret not yourself; it tends only to evil.
> For the evildoers shall be cut off,
>> but those who wait for the LORD shall inherit the
>>> land. (vv. 5–9 ESV)

David finally became king of Israel when he was thirty years old, and he reigned for forty long years. Saul was killed in battle a short time before by an enemy army.

David performed well in adversity, but he stumbled in prosperity. After he became king, he slept with another man's wife, got her pregnant, arranged for her husband's murder, and married her himself! (Please note: Even God's people can blow it—badly.) Confronted by a storytelling prophet named Nathan, David still had enough conscience left to condemn acts very similar to his own. Nathan's story of a man with many sheep who stole another man's only lamb highly offended him, and he called for the punishment of the supposed thief. When Nathan politely told David he was pointing the finger at himself, David was crushed:

> David said to Nathan, "I have sinned against the LORD." And Nathan said to David, "The LORD also has put away your sin; you shall not die. Nevertheless, because by this deed you have utterly scorned the LORD, the child who is born to you shall die." (2 Sam. 12:13–14 ESV)

David saw his sin as an affront to God. And because he loved God, he repented and ran to him for forgiveness. When we're God's children, we turn to God—even when we've betrayed him. David did not believe that his actions cut him off from God or that God was forever done with him. He believed he had sinned against a Father who loved him, and he sought forgiveness from the one he'd wronged.

He experienced the consequences of his sin, yes. But he was not abandoned by his God. Not ever.

Friend, your mistakes don't define you any more than your victories do. You and I are defined by what God says about us (all those wonderful things in Ephesians 2!), not what the world says. When we've messed up, when we've hurt ourselves or others by our own selfishness, we should run toward God, not away from him! When we need mercy, we should go where mercy is found:

Have mercy on me, O God,
    according to your steadfast love;
according to your abundant mercy
    blot out my transgressions.
Wash me thoroughly from my iniquity,
    and cleanse me from my sin!
For I know my transgressions,
    and my sin is ever before me.
Against you, you only, have I sinned
    and done what is evil in your sight,
so that you may be justified in your words
    and blameless in your judgment. . . .
Deliver me from bloodguiltiness, O God,
    O God of my salvation,
and my tongue will sing aloud of your righteousness.
    (Ps. 51:1–4, 14 ESV)

Even when he did wrong, David got it right. Those of us who belong to God can be just as confident as he was about the Father's steadfast love for us, about his good intent where we're concerned:

But I am like a green olive tree
    in the house of God.
I trust in the steadfast love of God
    forever and ever.
I will thank you forever,
    because you have done it.
I will wait for your name, for it is good,
    in the presence of the godly. (Ps. 52:8–9 ESV)

Two more big as-ifs help me to surrender myself daily to God. Maybe they'll help you too. I try to live as if his mercies really are "new every morning" (Lam. 3:22–23 ESV) and as if the end of all things is good and true, no matter how messy the meantime gets. Most of the psalms aren't written from the other side of hardship. Just the opposite! They're cries straight from the middle of distress and danger and doubt. That's what makes them so powerful! David counts on the mercy of God always being available to him, and I count on it too. He counts on the providence of God to weave all things—including hard things—together for his good and for God's glory (Rom. 8:28). So do I.

If my identity depended on how well I perform in my many roles—wife, mom, friend, coworker, writer, performer, musician, daughter—I'd be sunk every other day! My track record is more inconsistent than I'd like in every circumstance. I can see plenty of room for improvement.

If I didn't believe God would keep showing up in my life, that he'd keep on demonstrating his crazy-good mercy to me, I might become overwhelmed by life's trials. But I *do* believe it, so even when life gets crazy and I get a little lost, I press on by pressing into him. I believe him when he says I am his precious child, his workmanship, his beloved. And you should too.

Josie was three and the boys were two when I spoke at my very first mom's conference, dotMOM, in Nashville. I was asked to lead worship for the event and do a seminar as well, and I was excited about the trip. Any mom knows how much stuff you need to pack for three small children, right? I had gotten everything together and was doing my best to get us all out the door and into the van with plenty of time to spare. I thought I'd done a pretty good job, too, until I realized when we got there I'd left most of their stuff by the back door—in Atlanta. Their food. Their Pack 'n Play. Their clothes. Everything, really.

We'd hit the road while it was still dark, letting the kids sleep in their pajamas. We were going to dress them when we arrived at the church, but now we had nothing for them to wear. My piano player went looking for shoes for them in one place, and my manager was shopping for clothes in another. But once we had those things, plans changed again when one of the twins threw up. The kids spent the first half of the day in pajamas and shoeless. After the first music set, the Compassion International rep eyed my ragged crew, put his arm around me, and said, "If you want, we could make sponsorship packets for your three—and they, too, could have some shoes." It would have been funnier if it hadn't been so true.

The best—and truest—thing I could say to the moms gathered there that weekend was this: "No matter how good or not good you are at this, God is crazy about you. He loves you when you mess up just as much as he loves you when you get it right. Your identity is wrapped up in him, and he's made you worthy." Most days, thankfully, aren't as crazy as that one was. And most days, I manage to live out of his love and not out of my own critical self-assessment. It's a plan I highly recommend.

I Give Up

In the end, it won't matter that I didn't ace every day of being a wife or mom or teacher or performer. It will matter that I lived as if I believed what God says is true. Sometimes you just have to start by swallowing hard, saying "I will," and placing your trust in him:

Speak to me my heart is open
Speak to me here in this moment

Above distraction, above the noise
God let me hear Your voice

I will trust
I will cling
To every word You breathe
Every word You breathe
I am found
My soul set free
With every word You breathe
Every word You breathe

It's water for the thirsty
Power for the weak
Shelter for the weary
Help for those in need
It's revival for the broken
It answers those who seek
With every word You've spoken
You're bringing life to me
You are bringing life to me[1]

If believing him is a good beginning (and it is!), then acting on that belief, trusting it, and clinging to it is the best choice for you and me, every single time.

WHITE FLAG PRAYER #9

Father, I'm acting on the belief that you are who you say you are and that you can do what you say you can do, regardless of my circumstances. Amen.

PART FOUR

What Happens When I Surrender?

TEN

My Choices Impact Others

Our choices have consequences, some good and some not so good. For instance, when I choose to drive over the speed limit (not that this would *ever* happen), I risk being pulled over by an observant police officer and handed a speeding ticket. When I choose to eat more calories than I burn, I'm going to see my choice reflected in the numbers between my toes on the bathroom scale. When I choose to skip an early morning class and sleep in, my grade may reflect that decision. (Mom and Dad: this is purely theoretical. Of course, I never did this.) By the same token, if I choose to go to bed at a reasonable hour, I'm likely to have more energy the next day than I would have if I had pulled an all-nighter.

Some people call this the "law of cause and effect." The Bible calls it "reaping and sowing." I just call it *real life*. I can't think of a single decision you or I could make that wouldn't impact something—or someone—else. So when we choose surrender—when we stop trying to stiff-arm God or give him orders and begin saying yes to him instead—things change not just *within* us but *around* us. And for the good.

When we're convinced he knows and loves us and that he's going to keep his promises, surrendering our lives to him just makes more sense. Surrender requires us to let go, choose belief, and act "as if"—as if God is who he says he is, as if we are who he says we are, and as if he is always at work on our behalf.

But what about the *results* of our surrender? What really happens when we raise the white flag and give up control (or the illusion of it) to the Father who loves us?

I'll give you a hint: a lot. And very little of it happens *alone*. My relationship to God is never just a personal thing because my life is connected to a lot of other lives. And that's the way he meant for it to be.

I have those days when I imagine how great it would be to disappear to some isolated mountain cabin or beach house for a while and not see another living soul. Days when I'd like to have the grocery store aisles all to myself or be the only car at every light along my drive to work and back. I'm pretty sure we all do. But we're not created to live like hermits, shut off from the rest of the world. We're made for community.

The word *community* gets plenty of attention nowadays, but it's not a new concept. We read in Genesis how God quickly populated his creation with a community of two—Adam and Eve—and soon after that with their children and their children's children. He gathered an entire nation of people for himself beginning with Abraham and Sarah. That nation, Israel, was made up of twelve tribes, each descended from one of Jacob's twelve sons. Even Jesus was born into a family, grew up in a small town with friends and neighbors nearby, and later surrounded himself with a dozen men who were committed to his teaching and went everywhere with him.

But before Adam and Eve ever were, God existed in community. With himself. He has always existed as a three-person God: God the Father, God the Son, and God the Holy Spirit. God's identity as Father, Son, and Holy Spirit stretches my finite mind past the limits of its understanding, but I believe it.

Once upon a time I may have had some romantic idea that I would travel through life solo, with just a keyboard or a guitar. I'd write songs that came from my one-on-one relationship with God and sing them by myself to strangers.

Today if you pulled in my driveway, you'd be jockeying for parking space with a minivan and a small tour bus, dodging bicycles and tricycles in between. I'm making music, all right, but almost never alone. I get inspiration from seeing God move in the lives of others just as often as I do from seeing him move in my own.

Martin and I are solidly rooted and invested in our Perimeter Church community. These days we rarely have fewer than a half-dozen humans in our house at any one time. Sometimes the head count changes so fast I can't keep up! Now when I play and sing, it's most often just two miles down the road from our house, together with the body of believers that knows us best. You can't fool the friends who witnessed a two-year-old's meltdown in your living room the night before. They *know* you're not perfect and that your life gets just as messy as theirs.

When we make important decisions as a couple about our careers or our family, we rarely do it alone. We call in the big guns! Our friends and ministry colleagues have prayed with us and advised us in so many seasons of life: when we've struggled with whether to have a family, with the best ways to pattern our roles as husband and wife, with how to invest our time and choose our big outside commitments.

I honestly believe one of the worst lies the evil one spreads about marriage is that it's a union between two people, full stop. That it's "you and me against the world." We marry in the church not just to proclaim that God has brought us together and binds us together but that God will *hold* us together. He'll keep us together.

If Jesus is the center of a marriage between two believers, then the church is its outside binding. Not the building—the people. They're the ones who will keep you honest when your will is weak and your union is challenged. Because it will be. It makes me sad to see people who think of their marriage as only a relationship of two and who feel like failures if they can't manage to keep every aspect of it healthy by themselves. Neither of us—Martin nor me—imagines we're self-reliant, operating outside of a loving, supportive community.

I'll give you one example. Before we had Josie, Martin and I almost always traveled together, and we wouldn't have considered any other way of doing ministry. But the logistics got more and more complicated when a nanny, babies, and all their gear were added to the mix of musicians, instruments, and sound equipment. Martin's schedule was also disrupted each time he shut down what he was doing to go with me.

It was a tough decision to make, but we decided Martin and the kids wouldn't travel with me every time I hit the road. We enlisted our good friends to pray it through with us. In the end—helped by others—we came to see that our old way of handling touring needed to change, and we were able to make that change with plenty of caring advice and support.

Sure, we're two strong-minded, grown-up people who don't have to ask anyone else what to do. We don't need anyone's permission to make changes in our routine. But we've learned that there's wisdom in seeking counsel. In part because of our unique situation, Martin and I have come to understand the impact our seemingly small decisions can have on others, and we've definitely reaped the benefits of involving our community in some of those choices.

Part of my seminary training has been to study the history of great movements in the Christian church. That may sound like a hopelessly nerdy exercise, but it's actually given me great perspective in my work as a worship leader. The gospel never changes, and I thank the Lord for that! It is perfect and timeless and true for every age. But the ways of "doing church" have changed through the years, just like social norms and community practices tend to do.

Back in the frontier days of protestant Christianity in America, traveling evangelists like Charles Finney began preaching the importance of having a "personal relation-ship" with Christ. Finney experienced his own emotionally charged conversion as a twenty-nine-year-old attorney, and from that time on he urged others to accept Christ personally, openly, and publicly. His brand of revivalism paved the way for later evangelists like Dwight Moody, Billy Sunday, and Billy Graham, whose compelling invitations to receive Christ during public altar calls would shape the lives of millions.

Every single one of us *does* have a personal responsibility to respond to the claims of Christ. No one can do this for us. Jesus asked his closest followers for commitment. He went beyond "Who do people say that I am?" to "Who do *you* say that I am?" (see Matt. 16:13–20). We each must answer that same question for ourselves.

But that increased focus on individual response to the gospel has led some to come away with the idea that Christianity is a religion of and for individuals. It is not. Jesus calls the collective church his bride, not just me or you.

So when I hear things in worship like, "If you were the only person in the world, Jesus would have died for you," I cringe a little. Sure, that's true—but you *aren't* the only person in the world, and neither am I. No one else has been, either, since Eve was created for Adam. And when I hear worship leaders encourage congregants to "pretend there's no one here but you and God" or "close your eyes, block everyone else out, and get alone with God," I wonder, *Well, why did we all get up and drive to church, then? Shouldn't we just stay home?*

Sometimes I think we're guilty as a church of singing too many "I" songs and not enough "we" songs.

Sometimes we forget that God always meant for us to do this Christian life together.

Luke told us in Acts what community life was like in the early church, and the picture he painted is a beautiful one:

> And they devoted themselves to the apostles' teaching and the fellowship, to the breaking of bread and the prayers. And awe came upon every soul, and many wonders and signs were being done through the apostles. And all who believed were together and had all things in common. And they were selling their possessions and belongings and distributing the proceeds to all, as any had need. And day by day, attending the temple together and breaking bread in their homes, they received their food with glad and generous hearts, praising God and having favor with all the people. And the Lord added to their number day by day those who were being saved. (Acts 2:42–47 ESV)

Christ's first followers needed one another. They shared with each other. They ate together and worshiped together, and, as much as they were able, they served one another and met each other's immediate needs. And as they did those things, God made their number grow. They didn't focus on growth. They focused on God and on caring for those in their community out of the overflow of their love for him.

These people were Jews who had always had religion. They weren't attracting others to join them because they were "religious." Their numbers were increasing because of their distinctive community. The way they lived wasn't the norm of the day. And it wasn't just that their community was as attractive as their message: their community *was* their message, lived out every day in real, ordinary lives. They became the living embodiment of their astounding proclamation:

> Now the full number of those who believed were of one heart and soul, and no one said that any of the things that belonged to him was his own, but they had everything in common. And with great power the apostles were giving their testimony to the resurrection of the Lord Jesus, and great grace was upon them all. (Acts 4:32–33 ESV)

Jesus' first followers shared things that connected them physically. Their hearts and minds were bonded in ways that connected them spiritually. Their collective testimony about Jesus' resurrection was powerful—and their lifestyle was too. God was pouring out his grace on them in a big way.

Nothing in Scripture ever, ever points to the Christian life being lived out alone.

As we've already said, when we live in community our choices affect others. There's no way around it. The only question is *how.* Two familiar stories from the Bible suggest that decisions made by one person can have a powerful, positive, and lasting impact for many. And both of these stories involve surrender.

The first one still slays me every time I think of it.

How in the world could a young, teenaged girl have the courage and faith to say yes to an unthinkable plan that would change the course of her life forever? Maybe you have a daughter her age. Would you believe she was in any way prepared for such an assignment? Mary probably hadn't made a single big decision in her life (tradition says her parents would have selected Joseph for her as a husband) when she chose to say yes to an angel's surprise announcement.

Can you imagine how staggering this bit of news must have sounded to a sheltered girl from a small town, newly engaged to be married? Just picture this:

> In the sixth month the angel Gabriel was sent from God to a city of Galilee named Nazareth, to a virgin betrothed to a man whose name was Joseph, of the house of David. And the virgin's name was Mary. And he came to her and said, "Greetings, O favored one, the Lord is with you!" But she was greatly troubled at the saying, and tried to discern what sort of greeting this might be. And the angel said to her, "Do not be afraid, Mary, for you have found favor with God. And behold, you will conceive in your womb and bear a son, and you shall call his name Jesus. He will be great and will be called the Son of the Most High. And the Lord God will give to him the throne of his father David, and he will reign over the house of Jacob forever, and of his kingdom there will be no end." (Luke 1:26–33 ESV)

Today a typical fifteen-year-old girl like Mary might respond, "OMG. TMI." As in, "Oh, God! It's really you! And that's way too much information for any human being to grasp in one thirty-second sound bite!"

First, a blazing angel appears in your bedroom. Second,

he calls you by your name! Then he says God has noticed you, is pleased with you, and is with you. Woo, boy. Let that sit for a minute—or not. Because before you can take his greeting in, the angel blows you away with the news that you're about to become pregnant. Except that's not humanly possible, and you know it. And it's quite troublesome, given your recent change in relationship status.

But wait. There's more.

Your baby will be a boy, and God has his name already picked out: Jesus. Nothing about him will be ordinary. He will be great. He will be God's Son. And he'll rule a kingdom that will never end.

When the angel paused and gave Mary a chance to speak, she asked what must have been the first question that came to mind: *How? How is this going to happen? Because I'm a virgin—and virgins don't have babies. At least not where I'm from* (v. 34).

The angel spelled out more details of God's plan for her: "The Holy Spirit will come upon you, and the power of the Most High will overshadow you; therefore the child to be born will be called holy—the Son of God" (v. 35).

And Mary, little Mary full of grace, said simply, "Behold, I am the servant of the Lord; let it be to me according to your word" (v. 38).

Boom. Yes. Yes!

Mary surrendered to God's wild, inconvenient, shocking plan for her future because she knew God and considered herself his servant.

And you and I and who knows how many others throughout time and history have become the joyful beneficiaries of the blessing of her beautiful surrender. The ripple effect of her personal, private decision that day goes on and on and on. Today someone will trust Jesus and be reconciled to God because Mary said yes!

℃℈

The second story is the one of a man named Stephen.

Stephen attracted the attention of Jewish leaders in Jerusalem not long after Jesus' death and resurrection. Plenty of Jews in the city weren't fans of Jesus or his followers. They wished "the Way" would *go* away so they could go back to business as usual in their synagogues. But Stephen was a hard man to ignore. His unusual grace and power and the great signs and wonders he performed made him a threat to those who only wanted to maintain the religious status quo.

Before long, these men began spreading lies about him (much like they did about Jesus), stirring up the people against him. Stephen was seized and brought before the council of Jewish elders (does this sound familiar?), who had already lined up plenty of false witnesses willing to testify against him: "This man never ceases to speak words against this holy place and the law, for we have heard him say that this Jesus of Nazareth will destroy this place and will change the customs that Moses delivered to us" (Acts 6:13–14 ESV).

When Stephen was asked if the charges against him were true, he could have denied them. But he didn't. Instead he preached the gospel to his accusers—tracing God's history with his people from Abraham, Isaac, Jacob, Joseph, Moses, and David—all the way to Jesus.

He could have left well enough alone: just saying, "Jesus was God's messenger to us—just like these other men were." And that much would have been true. But the story didn't stop there, and neither did Stephen.

He reminded them that they had resisted God, rejected Moses, broken the law, and killed the prophets—all before murdering Jesus:

> "You stiff-necked people, uncircumcised in heart and ears, you always resist the Holy Spirit. As your fathers did, so do you. Which of the prophets did your fathers not persecute? And they killed those who announced beforehand the coming of the Righteous One, whom you have now betrayed and murdered, you who received the law as delivered by angels and did not keep it." (Acts 7:51–53 ESV)

Ouch.

Someone has said when you find yourself in a hole it's time to stop digging. But Stephen didn't think so. He dug even deeper, and he struck a nerve. His bold, Spirit-inspired sermon got him killed—stoned to death by the very audience he hoped to persuade.

Stephen didn't shade the truth or try to calm the powers that be. He understood the consequences of his words—he knew they would very likely cost him everything. But they were true and so worth saying that he spoke them anyway, hoping that someone would hear and believe.

He surrendered his life for the sake of the gospel story. His dying face, we're told, looked like the face of an angel (Acts 6:15)—and, as the rocks pounded him, he cried out,

"Lord Jesus, receive my spirit" and "Lord, do not hold this sin against them!" (Acts 7:59–60). Then he died.

Stephen put the cause of Christ before his own cause. He didn't seek justice for himself. He sought honor for Jesus. He surrendered his life for the highest good he knew—Jesus Christ, the Son of God.

And the church was changed forever.

One of those who witnessed Stephen's brutal murder was a young Jew named Saul . . . who became the zealous Christian convert and missionary Paul . . . who took the gospel to the Gentile world! Through Stephen's surrender, Christianity grew way, way beyond Jerusalem, and untold millions believed.

Maybe you're thinking that Mary and Stephen were exceptional people. Superstars of faith. Not like you and me. Maybe you believe that the only surrendered lives that have eternal impact are those of "hall of fame" believers, not ordinary people like us.

But you'd be wrong.

No one else will give birth to God's Son. That assignment was only for Mary. It will never happen again. And more than likely, you won't be called by God to become a martyr, giving your life for your belief in Christ. Some of us will. But not many. That privilege is for a precious, blessed few.

But every single one of us is called *daily* to show our love for God by saying yes to his plan and no to our own short-sighted agendas. And by the power of his Spirit, we can.

We can say yes to obedience. Yes to speaking the truth

in love. Yes to loving our neighbors as we love ourselves. Yes to sharing the good news. Yes to serving others. Yes to caring for the sick, the poor, the sorrowing. Yes to nurturing those who live closest to us—our husbands and children, our family and friends.

Our yeses won't look the same. But every surrender offered by you or me for the love of Christ can be fruitful in the kingdom. Maybe history won't be changed. But we will. And others will too.

My attitude of surrender changes me, my family, my church, and my community. The consequences of personal surrender can be far-reaching and lasting. In other words, I should be excited about what God can do through me when my heart is surrendered to him!

Here's what I know for sure: When I surrender, relationships can strengthen and grow. When I surrender, reconciliation is possible. When I surrender, I leave a legacy. And when I surrender, I am worshiping God.

WHITE FLAG PRAYER #10

God, I know my surrender to you is never solely personal—it affects my family, my church, and my community. Help me be a light and a blessing wherever I go. Amen.

ELEVEN

When I Surrender, Relationships Can Heal and Thrive

Martin and I were teenagers when we met. We'd weathered plenty of challenges together and seen one another grow through many different seasons of life before we married in our midtwenties. Because of that, I might have believed he couldn't surprise me and that we'd long ago ironed out whatever small differences we had.

But when you marry, you really do learn things about your mate that you never knew before. Things that don't make sense at all.

Like, maybe, the crazy way they fold laundry.

Everyone knows how to fold a T-shirt, right? Sides and sleeves in, bottom up, top over. Three perfect sections. Neat and easy.

I was shocked when I saw that Martin folded his T-shirts

(and mine) *lengthwise*, then in two. Which leaves a fold right down the middle of the shirt when you wear it! I know it sounds silly, but I wanted the shirts folded my way since my way was obviously better.

I demonstrated my superior technique for Martin and assumed that was that. Until the next time he did the laundry—and our shirts were folded *his* way.

I'm embarrassed to admit that this was ever an issue, but it was! And now here it is—forever in print.

Our standoff might have lasted longer than it did if I hadn't mentioned it to a married friend.

"Wait," she said. "Back up. Did you say Martin did the laundry?"

I did.

"He took it out of the dryer? And folded it?"

He did.

"And your problem is *what*?"

Oh, yeah. Right.

Our laundry conflict may sound small (and it was), but lots of "smalls" can get big over time if you let them. Learning to do the right thing in the little stuff is great practice for when the stakes get higher. Close relationships, like marriage, offer a boot camp–worthy training ground for surrender. You'll get chances to improve your skills every day.

And for the record—however my husband chooses to fold our shirts these days is fine with me. I wore my shirt with the crease down the front as a badge of honor and was even more honored to have a sweet husband who washed and folded it!

I know my God prizes surrender. The Bible tells me he does. In Psalm 51 David wrote,

> For you will not delight in sacrifice, or I would give it;
>   you will not be pleased with a burnt offering.
> The sacrifices of God are a broken spirit;
>   a broken and contrite heart, O God, you will not
>   despise. (vv. 16–17 ESV)

Straight up, God is pleased when I submit my will to his. When I recognize and confess my failures, he never despises me. He looks beyond my actions and sees into my heart. Every time.

Not only does God prize my surrender—Jesus models it. He shows me what it looks like to live my life surrendered to the will of God. He did it so that I can see the way it's done.

ℭ

Mothers want the best for their kids. It's natural. We just do. Still, I get a little embarrassed for the mother of Jesus' disciples James and John when I read her story in Matthew 20. One day she came to Jesus with her sons, knelt before him, and asked a big favor:

> She said, "Grant that one of these two sons of mine may sit
> at your right and the other at your left in your kingdom."
>   "You don't know what you are asking," Jesus said
> to them. "Can you drink the cup I am going to drink?"
>   "We can," they answered.

159

Jesus said to them, "You will indeed drink from my cup, but to sit at my right or left is not for me to grant. These places belong to those for whom they have been prepared by my Father." (Matt. 20:21–23 NIV)

When the other ten disciples heard what happened, they were not pleased. Smelling a rift in the ranks, Jesus called them all together and explained exactly how "getting ahead" happens in God's kingdom:

"You know that the rulers of the Gentiles lord it over them, and their high officials exercise authority over them. Not so with you. Instead, whoever wants to become great among you must be your servant, and whoever wants to be first must be your slave—just as the Son of Man did not come to be served, but to serve, and to give his life as a ransom for many." (Matt. 20:25–28 NIV)

Jesus, the one Mrs. Zebedee lobbied for privilege for her sons, was not willing to claim privilege for himself—and he was the Son of God! The role he voluntarily chose was not king but servant. How could his followers possibly demand a higher place for themselves? How can we?

In a few days' time, Jesus would back up his words with action, demonstrating for his disciples what it looked like to serve others in love. They were gathered in Jerusalem for Passover. That very night he would be betrayed and seized, questioned and condemned. Their time together was coming to a close. Jesus knew this. They did not.

Before anyone else could volunteer to perform such a

lowly duty, Jesus—their master and teacher—stripped down to the waist, took a towel and a basin, knelt, and began to wash the dirt from his disciples' feet, one by one.

Maybe because no servant was with them the disciples had hesitated, waiting to see who would lower himself to the necessary foot-washing task. None of them wanted to volunteer for the meanest job. Can you imagine how they must have felt when their leader beat them to it? Sure, Peter protested, but Jesus pressed on. He had a point to make.

> When he had washed their feet and put on his outer garments and resumed his place, he said to them, "Do you understand what I have done to you? You call me Teacher and Lord, and you are right, for so I am. If I then, your Lord and Teacher, have washed your feet, you also ought to wash one another's feet. For I have given you an example, that you also should do just as I have done to you. Truly, truly, I say to you, a servant is not greater than his master, nor is a messenger greater than the one who sent him. If you know these things, blessed are you if you do them." (John 13:12–17 ESV)

Not only did Jesus surrender his right to be honored as the king that he was, he surrendered his expectations of his followers—that they would show their love for him by attending to his needs. He met them where they were: proud, stubborn, demanding, needy. He willingly assumed the lowest rank—first for the love of his Father and then for their own good.

Friend, a role doesn't automatically equal a right. Maybe in the military a certain rank requires an automatic salute. Or the arrival of England's sovereign requires that the band strike up "God Save the Queen." But most of us aren't generals or royalty. Our relational roles don't necessarily entitle us to a life of preferential treatment, of always being considered first.

As far as I know, there's no frequent flyer club for wives that ensures automatic "niceness" upgrades for accumulated days of continuous service. And there's no blanket guarantee for mothers that says once you've changed so many poopy diapers you've achieved champion mom status.

In real life, relationships require a lot of grace applied over time, and they are almost always helped by an attitude of mutual surrender.

One of the results of Martin's illness is that he cannot legally drive. I won't lie: having only one adult in the house with a driver's license is challenging, but over time we've learned ways to work around it. Even though he can almost always get a ride anywhere he needs to go, I understand that's not the same as having the autonomy to get there by yourself.

Four or five years after his surgery a friend asked him if he'd ever thought about riding his bike as an alternative. He hadn't, and neither had I. Quite honestly, I wasn't crazy about the idea at all.

Martin has only 50 percent of his normal vision, and I didn't relish the idea of him becoming a splat on the road because of a car he didn't see in time. Sure, we only live two miles from the church where he does a lot of volunteering, but those two miles are heavily trafficked all day every day.

This was a huge deal for us. Obviously, we both longed for the freedom the bike would give Martin. But at the same time, I was concerned for his safety. How could we balance his need for independence with my desire to protect him? Ultimately, after a lot of prayer and discussion, we agreed to trust that God would give him the wisdom to make the right decision.

He chose to ride the bike, and he's still riding it. It's given him way more control over his schedule and his day. He's happy with the choice, and, so far, he's been quite safe. (He even bikes to the store sometimes to pick up things we need, which is an unexpected bonus!) But the bike is still an issue of surrender for me. Even though I trust him to be careful, I'd worry less if he didn't ride it. But mine wasn't the only surrender on the issue. Martin told me when he made his choice, "If you ever feel like this is an unsafe thing and you want me to stop, I will."

Neither of us insisted we were right and the other was wrong. Martin didn't say, "I'm the husband: my body, my bike, my choice." I didn't say, "I'm the wife and you promised to care for me and our children. How can you do that if you're hit by a car?"

He made the final choice, but he is willing to make a different choice if I ask him to. I know that, and, so far, I haven't.

We continue to be hopeful that advances in medicine or technology may one day improve Martin's disability. However, the process of working through the bike decision was a good one for us, and it helped us navigate other challenges where our opinions differ. It also taught us that we don't have to look far for opportunities for surrender—or even to go outside our own front door. There's plenty to work on right here with our relationships at home.

Parenting is another surrendering opportunity, where a role doesn't make a right. Martin and I have the responsibility to love and nurture our kids and teach them right from wrong. But we're not foolproof. We make mistakes. All parents do.

Once, when Ben and Griffin were still in diapers, I put them down for a nap in their room upstairs, then after about twenty minutes I heard them squealing and laughing. When I went up to check on them I almost wished I hadn't. They'd both pooped in their diapers, taken them off, and were in the process of "decorating" their room with the diapers' contents.

Their little brown handprints were everywhere: carpets, walls, furniture, each other—and they were still at it. Honestly, I didn't know whether to try and clean up their mess or just list the house for sale. (Or maybe hustle everyone outside and burn it down.) I was beside myself. I mean *beside* myself. Martin was off coaching a baseball game, so it was just me, no reinforcements.

I ran the bathtub full of soapy water, scrubbed them down, re-diapered and dressed them, then got everyone in the car to go rent one of those industrial-strength carpet cleaning machines. (Trust me. My upright wasn't going to handle this job.) Back home again, I settled them downstairs with a movie so I could figure out where to start on the room. I'd been up to my elbows in cleaning products and biting back tears for a good half hour when one of them came back upstairs.

"Mommy . . . Mommy."

"Sweetie, Mommy's busy. Can you go back downstairs and watch your movie please?"

"Mommy . . . Mommy!"

I turned around and looked at him.

"Do you want a pancake?"

Huh? Did I want a *what*?

"We made pancakes for you."

That didn't sound so good. I left the mess upstairs only to find a bigger (but less smelly) mess downstairs. Somehow the boys had gotten into the pantry, found the Bisquick, and tried to mix some up with a plastic play bucket full of water. On the carpet. Like you do. When you're two.

Man, two messes were one too many. I started wailing. I yelled at them. Grabbed the Bisquick box away from them and screamed and yelled some more. I mean, I really lost it. Somewhere between the poop and the pancakes I totally abandoned every ounce of maternal sanity I ever possessed. It was not a mom-blog worthy moment. I did not take a selfie and post it.

When I finally looked at them, my babies were both crying, up to their ankles in gooey "pancake batter."

Feeling like the biggest mom-flop in history, I hit the floor, pulled them both into my lap, and confessed.

"Boys, Mommy blew it. I should not have yelled at you. I know I scared you, and I'm sorry. Mommy's sorry. Mommy needs Jesus. Mommy needs grace."

We sat there for a while in the mess, just hugging each other.

Then I went for the teachable moment: "Now, is there anything *you guys* might need to apologize for?"

They couldn't think of anything, so I made some calm suggestions, then reminded them both of how much I love them. Because I do. Poop, pancakes, and all.

Parents like to maintain a stature of correctness—of always being right and never showing weakness. (I get that because I'm one.) But I can surrender that perfect persona for the sake of my kids and apologize when I'm wrong. They need discipline, and they get discipline. But they also need to know how much they're loved by the two flawed but well-meaning people they call Mom and Dad. We'll always be for them, no matter what.

One of the best things I can model for my kids is that when I blow it, I go to Jesus. And when we both blow it, we can surrender our pride and do that together.

Of all the ways we're called to surrender in our relationships, this one might be the hardest of all to pull off: surrendering the past.

Maybe there's a hurt in your past you just can't let go of, no matter how hard you try. Or a season you'd give anything to return to, but you can't. Maybe you're hanging on to the distant memory of a precious blessing and refusing to budge until God blesses you in the same way again. Or wishing you could erase the consequences of some sin long forgiven but not forgotten. At least not by you.

Here's what I've learned, and not the easy way: you can't grow beyond what you haven't grieved. Old hurts stuffed out of sight aren't healed. They're just hidden. The slightest pressure often forces them out of hiding.

Before we had Josie, we considered growing our family by adoption. We knew the path to biological children would be a tough one for us, and we had always been open to the idea of adopting. Friends who'd already navigated the process with agencies advised us that Martin's disability would likely keep us from being approved and that private adoption might be a better choice for us.

We began to pray about it and, in the meantime, were introduced by a friend to a young woman from my hometown who needed help. This girl had been through some terrible things and was all but alone in the world. We knew of a residential program our church supported that would be perfect for her, and we offered to help her to get in. It would provide her a safe place to live, counseling, and access to the tools she would need to become stable and independent. She was admitted to the program and moved to its center just a few miles from our home.

Not long after she arrived, she discovered that she was pregnant and told us she was not prepared to raise her child.

The timing seemed providential. Two months earlier, we hadn't known this girl; now we had already begun caring for her and (without knowing it) her baby. We asked God if adoption might be part of his plan for her and for us, and we felt the freedom to talk about it. Martin and I told her we would be willing to support her in the pregnancy and to adopt her baby at birth, and she said she would be thrilled for that to happen.

For the next two months we opened our home to her, helped her with the expenses of prenatal care, prayed with and for her, and had long conversations about what God might have in store for the future of this baby she was carrying. She never once expressed doubts about the adoption and encouraged our involvement in every way. Martin and I felt so hopeful, preparing our hearts and our home to become the parents of this baby.

Until we didn't.

First, we got word she had dropped out of the program, then we heard from a mutual friend that she had aborted her baby. Weeks ago. We got played. Hosed. And our hearts were broken. Not just that our dreams of beginning a family were crushed but that a precious life was lost and this vulnerable young woman was on her own again. We didn't even know where she was.

We found out about her abortion on a Friday. The next night I was on stage at Perimeter, playing the piano for a service for our church's newest parents, whose infant children were being welcomed into the life of the church. With a big smile on my face, I told them how happy I was for them. And I was. But that wasn't the whole story, not by a long shot.

A friend who knew what had just happened asked me, "Hey, was that hard for you?" And I was so emotionally numb that I actually denied the hurt by saying, "No. I'm trusting that God has a better plan." (At least I was trying to.)

I don't remember crying when I told Martin about the mother's abortion. It was a fact. A hard fact, but a fact. Maybe I was in shock, but for sure I wasn't processing what had happened to us in an honest way.

Over the following months I began to unravel. Before long, I emotionally shut down. I carried around this huge grief in my heart that my mind kept dismissing for the sake of survival. To get through the day, I needed *not* to go there. So I didn't. I tried instead to sweep my pain under the rug of my own spirituality. But the harder I tried, the more I hurt.

Before long, what I thought was just a little crack in my heart opened into a Grand Canyon. It wasn't only the loss of the baby we believed would be ours. It was the realization that I'd been emotionally "stuffing" for years. After Martin's surgery—when our life changed so drastically from what we imagined it would be—I never really grieved. I just powered through. And when things were hard between the two of us, I never told a soul. It felt wrong to me to say we were struggling when God had spared Martin's life.

On one level we'd been okay. We were committed to our marriage. We weren't falling apart. But we weren't really talking about what we'd lost, either. We weren't admitting how disappointed we were that our choices had narrowed; that our plans had been altered.

When I felt tired after a tough day at work, I didn't say so because I didn't want Martin to feel guilty that he did not have a job to go to. When we got home from a long road trip, I didn't say I wish I could have slept at least part of the way like Martin had because I knew he would rather have driven but couldn't. *Why open that can of worms*, I thought. *It wouldn't change anything.*

I somehow got it in my head that my role was load bearer and my job was to bear up. I was the one in our marriage with no physical limitations, so I had to be strong. I was the worship leader in our church, so I couldn't express my sadness or anger to God. Not while I was leading "How Great Is Our God" or "Indescribable" for a few thousand people every weekend. I hadn't learned how to lament.

I was trapped in a deep well of grief and ignoring every rope that might have helped me to climb out. What I needed was to surrender my pain to God and give him the opportunity to heal me.

On a walk through our neighborhood one day, listening to worship music, I dared to peek inside my soul, and what I saw was a big, ugly, gaping wound. I started to cry, and it felt like I didn't stop for months. For years after Martin's surgery I had barely shed a tear, but after this latest loss all those stored-up tears seemed to come pouring out.

I cried with Martin. And with friends. At staff meetings. And in worship. And you know what? It felt good. There were times I didn't even bother to apologize for my tears or wipe them away. I just let them fall.

I fed on God's Word in that season in a way I never have before or since. I ingested it. Memorized it. Savored it. It wasn't a luxury. It was a matter of life and death. I needed to hear what my Father had to say like I needed to breathe.

Psalm 43 became a lifeline of hope and promise for me:

> Vindicate me, O God, and defend my cause
>   against an ungodly people,
> from the deceitful and unjust man
>   deliver me!
> For you are the God in whom I take refuge;
>   why have you rejected me?

Why do I go about mourning
because of the oppression of the enemy?
Send out your light and your truth;
let them lead me;
let them bring me to your holy hill
and to your dwelling!
Then I will go to the altar of God,
to God my exceeding joy,
and I will praise you with the lyre,
O God, my God.
Why are you cast down, O my soul,
and why are you in turmoil within me?
Hope in God; for I shall again praise him,
my salvation and my God. (ESV)

My soul was in a dark place, and I couldn't always find my way to God. But this psalm said, "You don't have to get to me, Laura. I will get to you. My light and my truth will bring you where you need to be." And they did.

The light of God and the truth of God—his understanding, his loving-kindness, his promises, his mercy—came to me as friends when I let down my guard and gave it all up. They led me to his house. To his people. To the church. Being in his presence didn't send my heart into hiding anymore. It called me out. Instead of dreading Sundays when I knew I should be "on," I lived for them because I knew I wasn't "on"!

Ironically, the loss of this child let me be *his* child again. And slowly, by surrendering my hurt to him, I began to heal and hope.

Friend, hear this—we can't grow beyond what we can't

grieve. First before God, then with those who love us and love him together *with* us. So I'm asking: Is there a sorrow you need to grieve and surrender? A hurt from your past that needs to see the light of day so that you can inch ahead toward hope? An abuse from someone you trusted? A mistake you made that you can't get past? The death of a dream? A sickness or disability that changed the course of your plans? This matters so much. I'll wait right here while you remember.

Down to my bones I believe these words and can sing them now in any season:

> Hold fast my heart in trouble's wake
> My faith is small, but my God is great
> And You said you would be near the broken
> On my loneliest of days, I am never alone
> And I know you will bring peace
> Surpassing what my mind can know
> So steady now my weary soul
> O love that never lets me go
> When it feels like hope cannot be found . . .
> Grace abounds.[1]

Jesus set the ultimate standard for loving submission in obedience to the Father. Hours before he surrendered his life for us on the cross, he surrendered his will to the Father in the Garden of Gethsemane. "Not my will but thy will be done," he prayed, but not without a struggle (see Luke 22:42). When we follow his lead and surrender our will to his, God is pleased and honored—and our relationships can heal and thrive. Surrendered to him, I'm able to let go of my need to be right, to be first, to be served by others *my* way. And that's a very good thing.

WHITE FLAG PRAYER #11

God, I surrender to you my regrets, failures, and need to be right, especially in my relationships with those closest to me. Walk with me through grieving the dark places and into a new place of love, joy, and peace. Amen.

TWELVE

When I Surrender, Reconciliation Is Possible

Martin and I both grew up in the South, and when you grow up in Georgia or South Carolina or Alabama—actually anywhere from Texas to Florida and on up to Tennessee—you're exposed to plenty of good old SEC football. We deeply and sincerely believe there's no better college football played anywhere on the planet.

Die-hard fans of SEC football are crazy about their schools and aren't shy about showing it. Team flags fly in front of neighborhood homes, license plates announce loyalties, school colors are sported by everyone from toddlers to great-grandparents, and stadium crowds the size of small towns gather to cheer their teams on, week after week. Southern brides have even been known to consult football schedules before selecting their wedding dates, and babies are regularly named after beloved players and coaches.

We were Georgia Bulldog fans at my house growing up. University of Georgia football was sacred to my family. I've gone to UGA games since I was a kid, singing the fight song, ringing the Chapel Bell, and standing in The Arch between North Campus and downtown Athens. But I know that if you're a Texas A&M Aggie, you learn to sing the War Hymn and practice the Midnight Yell, and if Auburn's your school you greet your friends with "War Eagle" and roll Toomer's Corner after a big win.

It sounds a little crazy, I know, but your team is your team, and if you're a fan around here, you're a full-on fan. You identify with everything about your school. Their victories become your victories. Their rivals become your rivals. You're not ashamed of your over-the-top enthusiasm. You revel in it. You're happy to submit your individual preferences to the traditions and loyalties of your alma mater.

Because you've found your tribe.

God has a tribe too. He has a people. Those of us who follow Christ are a part of his crazy-big, extended, diverse, and eternal family. God's family tree transcends divisions of race, economics, education, and politics. Because it's not about that stuff. It's all about him.

God draws us to himself, and no matter what our personal differences might be, they matter way less than our love for him. In his tribe, that's how we roll. When we surrender to him, we assume his family likeness and adopt his agenda as our own. What matters to him matters to us. What angers him angers us. What he values, we value too. Including one another. He shows us how.

Imagine this. You've grown up in small town as a Jew who attends your local synagogue faithfully. Each time you gather you hear the Scriptures read—the books of Moses, the prophets—and together with your fellow Jews you pray for a promised Messiah to come and save your people.

One day another local, a young man you've known since childhood, stands up in the synagogue to read. The elders hand him the scroll of the prophet Isaiah. He unrolls it, finds his place, and with a clear voice says:

> "The Spirit of the Lord is upon me,
> because he has anointed me
> to proclaim good news to the poor.
> He has sent me to proclaim liberty to the captives
> and recovering of sight to the blind,
> to set at liberty those who are oppressed,
> to proclaim the year of the Lord's favor."
> (Luke 4:18–19 ESV)

The reader sits down, and every eye in the room is on him. What he says next is a game-changer: "Today this Scripture has been fulfilled in your hearing" (Luke 4:21 ESV).

When Jesus announced his identity and began his public ministry, he announced his agenda too. It was taken straight from the words of the prophet Isaiah. The Jews were expecting a deliverer for *the Jews*. God's plan was much broader than that.

Jesus came to bring good news to the poor, including those who were poor in spirit. To proclaim liberty to the captives, including those caught in the web of their own sin. He intended to bring sight to the blind, including those blinded by their own self-righteousness. And he meant to set free all those who were oppressed by injustice, not just first-century Jews oppressed by Rome.

The deliverance God promised was far bigger and more inclusive than anyone had imagined. This news did not go over well. When Jesus pointed out that God had never confined himself to working just among the Jews, those gathered that day in the synagogue were so offended they chased him to the edge of town and tried to throw him off a cliff!

Pastor and theologian John Piper has said that to be a Christian is to get up in the morning and go to bed at night dreaming not about how to increase our own comfort but how to advance God's cause.[1] That means loving what God loves and hating what God hates. It means welcoming those whom Christ welcomed and even being willing to offend those whom Christ offended.

And it means laying down our own agendas, with their petty judgments and secret prejudices and comfortable preferences, for his.

In early 2018, our lead teaching pastor at Perimeter Church, Randy Pope, began a sermon series he titled "Greater Love." For several weeks, our mostly white, suburban congregation explored together what the Bible has to say about loving others the way God loves—in particular, loving others of different races and beliefs and cultures.

The subject of race in our country has never been an easy one. Not 150 years ago and certainly not today. Randy knew the series would be emotionally charged and that his words would leave him vulnerable to all kinds of misunderstanding. He knew not everyone in our congregation would feel comfortable. All of us on staff understood that some folks would resist hearing the topic of racial reconciliation addressed from the pulpit. But we believed with Randy and our teaching team that God was calling us as a church to address it.

Several things stood out for me in that season of convicting biblical teaching. One was my pastor saying, "I will not use my advantages to maintain someone else's disadvantage, and I will not remain silent when I see this happen." Another was him confessing, "I regret deeply that I never preached this sermon forty years ago. Or thirty years ago, or twenty. Shame on me."[2] Failing to do what we know is right, he said, can be just as damaging as doing what is wrong.

Our entire church was encouraged to do two things as a result of this teaching. First, we were encouraged to repent of our own sins of prejudice, along with those of our fathers. And we were shown that a biblical precedent for this kind of confession exists.[3] Second, we were exhorted to intentionally seek out and form relationships with those who were different from us.

It's been said that 11:00 a.m. on a Sunday morning is the most segregated hour in America. We decided that we did not want to be "that church." Instead we wanted to proclaim ourselves as members of the team or tribe of God by showing love for one another, regardless of our external differences.

I saw a powerful example of this not long ago.

I watched *Mister Rogers' Neighborhood* as a child. It ran for more than thirty years and taught generations of children the simple value of being a good neighbor. Mr. Rogers tackled tough subjects like death, divorce, and anger with songs and hand puppets and trolleys in the Neighborhood of Make-Believe. With its uber-understated star, no one expected the show to be the hit it was, but kids loved Mr. Rogers. I did too.

A recent documentary of Fred Rogers's life, called *Won't You Be My Neighbor?*, included a powerful lesson from the series—one that aired in 1969, before I was born. That year, in the throes of the Cold War, the civil rights movement, political assassinations, and the Vietnam War, Episode 1065 revolved around two men and a tiny wading pool.

François Clemmons, an opera singer who Fred Rogers first saw perform in his hometown Pittsburgh church, joined the cast of *Mister Rogers' Neighborhood* in 1968 as Officer Clemmons. He was the first African American with a recurring role in a children's television series, and he was Rogers's off-screen friend as well.

Episode 1065 opens with Mr. Rogers talking about how hot the weather has been and how good it would feel to soak his feet in some cool water. Moving from his living room to the front yard, he slips off his shoes and socks, rolls up his pant legs, and slides his feet into a plastic baby pool filled with water from a garden hose.

Soon Officer Clemmons strolls by, and Mr. Rogers invites him to cool off his own feet in the pool. He gives his friend his chair, fetches another, and both men—one black and one white—sit and soak their bare feet together. They reminisce about their childhood days and enjoy a few relaxing moments chatting together before Officer Clemmons says he needs to get back to work.

He pulls his feet out of the pool, and Mr. Rogers is ready to dry them with his own towel. "Here," he says to his friend, "let me help you."

And just like that—Fred Rogers, a white, former Presbyterian minister turned unlikely television star, demonstrates a simple act of kindness in *complete* contrast to the current-day national culture of segregated pools, drinking fountains, public schools, and restaurants.

He let his actions speak. And those actions were visibly Christlike and powerfully countercultural. When Fred Rogers shared his wading pool with François Clemmons and dried his friend's feet, he was publicly rebuking racism through servanthood. He was showing his viewers how a simple act could build a bridge to someone whose skin was a different color.

This is how reconciliation can happen. Thousands upon thousands of children watched and learned.

Surrendering our agendas to God's agenda involves not just letting our actions speak but also letting our judgment go and leaving our premade labels at home.

I can't think of two groups more different from and opposed to one another than the Jewish Christians who made up the early church and their Gentile neighbors. The

Jerusalem Jews were a pretty homogenous group. They had similar backgrounds, had grown up with the same teachings, and were used to the same kind of worship. Sure, it was a big deal for them to embrace Christianity, but they did it *together*, from the same starting point.

Very soon Gentiles—non-Jews—began to embrace the message of the gospel too. It's impossible for us to understand how much the Jews hated the Gentiles. They called them "dogs" and considered them unclean. They avoided them in public, thanking God daily that they weren't born Gentiles.

Those biases were challenged when God directed the apostle Peter in a dream to change his views and consider things he'd always viewed as "unclean" to be "clean." Soon after the dream, Peter was visited by a messenger from a Roman centurion named Cornelius, who summoned him to his home. Peter went and told Cornelius,

> "You yourselves know how unlawful it is for a Jew to associate with or to visit anyone of another nation, but God has shown me that I should not call any person common or unclean. So when I was sent for, I came without objection. I ask then why you sent for me." (Acts 10:28–29 ESV)

Cornelius told Peter he'd also had a dream—that a man called Simon Peter had an important message for him and he should call Peter to his home. Cornelius was a devout man who feared God, but he knew nothing about Jesus. When Peter told him the story of Jesus, he and his entire household believed—along with everyone else who heard!

It seems like the church at Jerusalem never fully

embraced the idea that salvation was for everyone, including Gentiles—even though they eventually agreed with Peter that it was. The number of Gentile believers grew supernaturally at Antioch and expanded even more when Paul began to travel throughout the Greek and Roman world with the good news.

Peter surrendered his bias and became a part of that great Gentile wave's beginning, but he had to leave his prior judgments and negative labels at home to do so. He proved that enemies and rivals *can* become brothers—but only when they submit to an authority greater than themselves.

Remember when I told you I was a University of Georgia fan? Can you imagine my complete shock when I got to Perimeter Church in Atlanta and discovered that I was going to be working side by side with graduates from the University of Alabama? Goodness! I didn't know when I was a kid that people who went to Alabama could be Christians, much less pastors!

I had to let those old biases go, though, for the good of the gospel. (And now that I think of it, they may have had to let their prejudices about girls from Dawg Nation go too.)

Those of us who follow Jesus must be willing to blow up any rivalry that competes with the gospel and then make new connections in *his* name.

If you think reconciliation is just for those who hold giant prejudices against whole people groups, your view is too small. We all hold biases or grudges of the personal and private sort, and we need to let those go as well. We've all wronged someone. No one gets through this life with a perfect score. And the best time to seek reconciliation with our brothers and sisters in Christ is *as soon as possible*. At the first available opportunity.

I'm speaking from personal experience here.

When I came to Perimeter to work with our church's worship team, I had way more experience playing with hired professionals than I did working with a team of volunteer musicians. And it showed. I made a ton of rookie mistakes before I understood that shepherding the hearts of these hard-working volunteers was as much a part of my calling as helping them make great music for the morning service. Bottom line, I was a twenty-five-year-old kid trying to lead a group of people who were far more mature than me in a context I wasn't used to. I didn't know what I didn't know.

One of the musicians on our team was a very talented instrumentalist whom I seemed to rub the wrong way from the start. I don't even remember the specific circumstances now, but I know we butted heads more than a few times. I'm sure I did not relate to her with the respect that I should have, and my attitude hurt her feelings.

I was aware of the friction between us, but I was unsure how to address it. So I took the easy way out and did nothing.

When her husband was transferred for his job, she and her family announced they were moving. Across the Atlantic. Honestly, I think I breathed a sigh of relief. I may have even figured, "Well, she's moving halfway across the globe, so there's no point in trying to reconcile our differences now. Maybe this is God's way of getting us both past a very uncomfortable, awkward situation." (I said I need to grow, didn't I?)

Even after she left, though, this team member still kept coming to mind. She was a godly wife and mom I had a ton of respect for, and I continued to feel uneasy about the fact that nothing had been resolved. Somehow I let the geographic distance that had opened between us become an excuse for not making that humbling phone call I knew I should make. But just because you don't see someone on a regular basis does not mean reconciliation is no longer possible—or right.

Fast-forward a year, and God was still bringing her to my mind. Martin, Josie, and I took a trip to Europe and planned to spend a few days in Italy. This family did not live in Italy, but one afternoon, walking through a crowded Italian piazza, I heard someone call, "Laura, Laura!"

There's probably at least a dozen Lauras in this plaza right now, I thought, and I kept walking.

Then I heard, "Laura! Laura Story Elvington!" No mistake there.

When I looked in the direction of the voice, I saw the woman I'd been thinking of for months. If we'd known we were in the same city at the same time, we probably couldn't have found one another. But God in his providence took good care of that.

We stood and talked for a few minutes, and I remember saying to her, "Man, it's so great to see you again." And it was! There wasn't a chance for an extended private conversation that day, but the ice was broken. We'd connected again, and I knew it was no accident.

When I got home I wrote her an email. I told her how very sorry I was for the tension that had developed between us and the ways my selfish attitude and my thoughtlessness had wounded her. I should have apologized before she left and didn't. Instead God spent almost a year preparing my heart for our *next* meeting, halfway around the world.

Reconciliation isn't something you do only when it's convenient or comfortable. It's an action that's close to the heart of God, and the time for it is whenever the opportunity presents itself. I learned that day in Italy that when God tees it up, we need to hit the ball! This family has since moved back to Atlanta and rejoined our church, and I delight in seeing her each Sunday. I'm so grateful that God in his great mercy prepared a way for us to reconcile before that day ever came!

Maybe you get discouraged when you see anger and discord all around you. I know. I do too. We witness a flood of venom, incivility, and rudeness these days just by watching the first five minutes of the news! Everywhere I look I seem to find examples of outright hatred and injustice. The need for reconciliation is overwhelming in almost every area of contemporary life.

The thought of trying to address these enormous challenges can leave an ordinary person paralyzed. They seem too big. Too widespread. What good can one person do, after all? How can you or I hope to stem the tide of hatred that seems to flood over us, day in and day out?

Well, we can surrender our resistance to change. However small or insignificant it may seem, the opportunity before us is the one thing we can seize. It may be just apologizing to your husband or best friend about the thoughtless thing you said to them. It might be reaching out to a new neighbor whose belief, skin color, or political bent is different from yours. Start where you are—but start!

If you're a member of God's tribe, if you identify with his team, you'll prize reconciliation like he did—and does. God pulled off the greatest reconciliation in all of history when he brought a sinful world back to himself through the cross of his Son, Jesus Christ. Explaining this to the church at Colossae, Paul wrote:

> And you, who were dead in your trespasses and the uncircumcision of your flesh, God made alive together with him, having forgiven us all our trespasses, by canceling the record of debt that stood against us with its legal demands. This he set aside, nailing it to the cross. (Col. 2:13–14 ESV)

We're reconciled people—and all the better for it! How can we not be reconcilers ourselves? Because we are his tribe, we willingly adopt his agenda and lay aside, actually *surrender,* our old loyalties. He's made us that new:

> Therefore, if anyone is in Christ, he is a new creation. The old has passed away; behold, the new has come. All this is from God, who through Christ reconciled us to himself and gave us the ministry of reconciliation; that

is, in Christ God was reconciling the world to himself, not counting their trespasses against them, and entrusting to us the message of reconciliation. Therefore, we are ambassadors for Christ, God making his appeal through us. We implore you on behalf of Christ, be reconciled to God. For our sake he made him to be sin who knew no sin, so that in him we might become the righteousness of God. (2 Cor. 5:17–21 ESV)

One more thing: we'll be together as God's family for eternity—but God wants us to embrace that unity here and now. In the Lord's Prayer, Jesus taught his disciples to pray, "Thy kingdom come, Thy will be done, on earth as it is in heaven" (Matt. 6:9–13 RSV). He longs for us to live now on earth as we will live one day in heaven. The unity we achieve in this life will be made beautifully complete when we are together with him forever:

After this I looked, and behold, a great multitude that no one could number, from every nation, from all tribes and peoples and languages, standing before the throne and before the Lamb, clothed in white robes, with palm branches in their hands, and crying out with a loud voice, "Salvation belongs to our God who sits on the throne, and to the Lamb!" (Rev. 7:9–10 ESV)

Because we've been reconciled to God through Christ, you and I should make the first move toward the surrender of reconciliation right where we are. In your neighborhood. In mine. In your church. In mine. In your family or circle of friends. And in mine. Whatever the conflict might be, it's hard to go wrong when you lead with love.

WHITE FLAG PRAYER #12

God, forgive me when I've failed to initiate reconciliation with another. Help me become a peacemaker. Amen.

THIRTEEN

When I Surrender, I Leave a Legacy

We've seen how surrender changes us and how it can change others through us. But did you know the way we live our lives in submission to God can also affect lives in the generations that come after us? It can. Because our surrender leaves a legacy.

A song-writing friend and I were working on some ideas for new music. Because we're both the parents of young children, we were talking about what we hope to pass on to our kids, what kind of legacy we want to leave for our daughters and our sons after we're gone. Neither of us will leave a fortune behind. We don't have "trust fund babies" who'll inherit millions. But we both agreed we wanted to leave our children with a rich, deep, lasting inheritance of trust in Jesus.

The bottom line is this: I long for my children to inherit my faith in God. Of course, the decision to follow Jesus is theirs and theirs alone. Just like I can't guarantee Josie would play my old guitar or my string bass one day if I left them to her, I can't *insist* my kids embrace the generational legacy of faith in our families.

But I *can* do everything in my power to create an environment where it would be easy for them to choose it. God willing, our lives—Martin's and mine—will show our little ones how beautiful and desirable a life surrendered to God can be. Do they catch us on our knees before the Lord? Are they waking up to find me with my Bible open, stealing precious time with him? Do they see us as a family sharing with those in need?

Trust me, they're watching. And you're being watched too—whether you have kids or not. We're always handing down something, being followed by others, and I don't mean on Facebook. My six- and four-year-olds eyeball my every move. They're learning from me all the time, whether I'm crawling through stop-and-go Atlanta traffic at rush hour (careful, there, Mom!) or cooking a meal or singing a song. They see. They're observing what I do and taking it in. And as a side note, if you ever have trouble remembering something you've said, I highly recommend doing life with a three-year-old, because they seem to remember every word. I recently heard Griffin on his play phone asking an imaginary friend to watch his kids while he went to play a concert!

I walked into the living room not long ago and witnessed Ben and Griffin making "music" on a play drum set and keyboard, both dressed in coonskin caps and singing at the top of their lungs. I've been trying for weeks now to figure out what they should call their group: The Frontiersmen?

Crockett & Boone? The Coonskin Twins? (Actually, The Wailers would be pretty descriptive too.) They've got a mama who makes music, and they've been around it all their young lives, so they already do a pretty mean imitation of a boy band!

Not long after Timothy was born, I was in Josie's room with the two of them. One of the boys yelled for me from the bathroom, and I laid the baby on the bed with his sister to go give their brother a hand. (Oh, the joys of the potty-training years!) When I got back to her room, Josie was snapping Timothy into his onesie with a fresh new diaper. (Big sister has seen her share of diaper changes.)

"He was a little fussy," she said matter-of-factly, "so I changed him."

I thanked her, then she smiled and said, "When he grows up and someone asks him who his mommy is, he'll say, 'Which one—the big one or the little one?'"

I don't doubt that for a minute.

Friend, we're teaching with our lives, whether we mean to or not. Every single one of us. Every day.

❧

A long time ago, I decided on a few key values I wanted to model for my family as a wife and a mother. I may not hit the nail on the head every time, but I do have a plan. We've adopted it as our family code—goals written out on a plaque and hanging on a wall in our home.

No matter what kind of craziness we might encounter, we aim to choose joy and to let that joy show. Life's full of big and small challenges we don't expect or necessarily want. We can't always order our circumstances, but we can point our hearts toward joy. Instead of taking our emotional cues from what's going on around us, we can look to Jesus and find our joy in him.

I can't even think about legacy-making without thinking of the life of Christ. To say that Jesus left us a great legacy is a tremendous understatement. Did you know that hours before his death, Jesus was talking to his disciples about their joy? He was. In John's gospel we read Jesus' last words of instruction to these twelve men he loved. He spoke of the coming of the Holy Spirit to comfort them, of the importance of loving one another, and of their need to abide in him (John 14–15).

What end goal inspired him to focus on these things? Their joy: "These things I have spoken to you," he told them, "that my joy may be in you, and that your joy may be full" (John 15:11 ESV). The joy Jesus speaks of is *his* joy. He offers it. We receive it. He stirs it up in our hearts. We respond to it.

Before Martin and I were married, I went on a mission trip to Mongolia. At the time I was studying music at the University of South Carolina and didn't have a clue where my life was headed. I wasn't in a particularly solid place personally or spiritually. Mongolia is not the mission destination for you if you're fond of four-star hotels and haute cuisine. It's a bit more rugged than that.

All the things back home that made day-to-day life easy were missing in Mongolia. There, I had only two changes of clothes. I was tired and dirty most of the time. We ate mutton for breakfast, mutton for lunch, and mutton for dinner. One day, after I'd washed our entire team's dirty socks for the umpteenth time and hung them up on a clothesline strung between two yurts, it hit me: *I'm content here. I have no idea what tomorrow is going to look like, but I want to serve Jesus for the rest of my life. I've never felt this much joy!*

And *he* was the reason why. In his presence there really is fullness of joy. And in his right hand there really are pleasures forever (Ps. 16:11).

Our family prizes and tries to model kindness to others, especially those who are somehow different from us. Listen, I get that being self-centered is the most natural thing in the world for children. I understand empathy is a learned behavior. But it can be learned—or better yet, caught.

I'm thinking of a recent Monday afternoon in the carpool line, waiting to pick up Josie. We'd been on the road to Greenville, North Carolina, played a 7:00 p.m. show the night before, and driven straight back to Atlanta in time for school the next morning. I woke the kids up in our driveway at 5:00 a.m., got them bathed and dressed, then off to class on time. (Then mommy took a nap. A long one.)

That afternoon, I watched as Josie walked to our car with her teacher by her side. I rolled my window down for what I was sure was going to be a disapproving report of my tired girl, falling asleep in her classroom.

"Can I speak with you for a minute, please?" she asked.

Uh-oh. Here we go.

"Of course," I said, smiling brightly. "What's up?"

"I want to brag on your little girl for a second," she said. "There's a boy in her class who has ADHD. Josie has just gravitated toward him. She's always helping him; she stands with him in line when the other kids ignore him. I don't know what you've done to teach her to have such a heart of compassion for someone with learning differences, but it's just amazing."

I breathed a sigh of relief and thanked her for those encouraging words. "I don't know if you know this," I said, "but Josie's dad has a disability, so her sensitivity isn't something she's learned from a book or that we've intentionally taught. She's seen it up close, in real life. At home."

As we drove away I thought, *We would not send a child to a class to learn kindness any more than we would send them to a class to learn how to depend on God!* It's them being in that circumstance that helps them to learn, as well as seeing us respond to those challenges day in and day out.

It was good for me to hear that one of the things we were most concerned about when we began to pray about having children had—in God's hands—become a blessing in their lives we had not expected. We were wondering if we'd be able to "work around" Martin's disability—never even considering how God might work *through* it for our children's good!

I love that our sweet girl is not afraid to reach out to others who are different. She's brave and open and curious and kind. When she was four, she and I traveled with Compassion International to Guatemala. I've sponsored children with Compassion for more than twenty years now, and I chose to sponsor a young Guatemalan girl Josie's age so that the two of them could become pen pals. The opportunity for us to visit that country together was just too good to pass up, and she was super excited to see the place where her friend lived.

Participants on this trip who were sponsors were encouraged to spend a day in the life of a Compassion child, visiting their home and meeting their family. Josie helped a sponsored Guatemalan child do chores in the one-room, dirt-floor shack where she lived, and she stuck like glue to her all day long. The outdoor potty threw her a little at first, but she quickly got the hang of it and breezed through the kind of day that might have paralyzed a grown-up with fear.

I can "preach" to my kids all day long about the equality of genders, races, and socioeconomic classes, but children learn best by going and doing—just like grown-ups! Josie discovered that we have far more in common than our differences might suggest as she sat side by side with her new friend, making pictures together with crayons and paper.

Finally, we want our legacy to our children to include a fierce dependence on God. We don't hide our needs from them or pretend we've got everything under control 24/7. We let them see us ask God for help in all kinds of ways. They know they can depend on us, sure. But they also know that, as a family, we depend on God.

When Timothy's cleft lip and palate was detected in utero, there was nothing we could do to help him. We couldn't fix it—the only thing we could do for him was pray. Those kinds of situations can lead us to feelings of discouragement and defeat or to a place of hopeful dependence on God. Josie, Ben, and Griffin saw Martin and me pray for Timothy's healing and trust God to care for him. It's a little scary as a parent to think that our kids will learn this from us. We must be in a place of trust to model dependence on God for our children. Our dependence on him will help them to depend on him too.

We all need something to aim for. I don't want to get to the end of my life and be surprised by what I've left behind. These things are part of my plan for daily surrendering to God's authority and helping my family do the same. Psalm 145 offers a glimpse of King David considering his legacy and tipping his hand on *his* plan. He wrote:

> I will extol you, my God and King,
>> and bless your name forever and ever.
> Every day I will bless you
>> and praise your name forever and ever.
> Great is the LORD, and greatly to be praised,
>> and his greatness is unsearchable.
> One generation shall commend your works to another,
>> and shall declare your mighty acts.
> On the glorious splendor of your majesty,
>> and on your wondrous works, I will meditate.
> They shall speak of the might of your awesome deeds,
>> and I will declare your greatness.
> They shall pour forth the fame of your abundant
>> goodness
>> and shall sing aloud of your righteousness.
> (vv. 1–7 ESV)

David determined to praise and exalt his God, no matter what. He was going to extol, bless, and praise the name of God then and into eternity because God's character inspired this. He is worthy. We see David's sense of passing on something valuable when he acknowledged, "one generation shall commend your works to another, and shall declare your mighty acts." In other words, we each must tell the story of God's goodness and love to the ones who will come after us.

So David said, "I will praise God." I will offer up to God words that describe his worth because he deserves them.

For himself, David said he intended to meditate on the handiwork of God: "on the glorious splendor of your majesty, and on your wondrous works, I will meditate" (v. 5). He continued:

> The LORD is faithful in all his words
> and kind in all his works.
> The LORD upholds all who are falling
> and raises up all who are bowed down.
> The eyes of all look to you,
> and you give them their food in due season.
> You open your hand;
> you satisfy the desire of every living thing.
> The LORD is righteous in all his ways
> and kind in all his works.
> The LORD is near to all who call on him,
> to all who call on him in truth.
> He fulfills the desire of those who fear him;
> he also hears their cry and saves them.
> The LORD preserves all who love him,
> but all the wicked he will destroy. (vv. 13–20 ESV)

These are the things about God I'm going to commit to memory, David told himself: God's faithfulness. The way he lifts his people up. How he provides for our needs and sat-isfies our desires. His righteousness and kindness. The way he comes near when we call on him and preserves those of us who love him.

Can you imagine what our lives might look like (and the lives of others) if we filled our minds with thoughts like these? David left a legacy of prayer and praise to God for others to imitate. For ages these inherited psalms have shaped the public worship and private devotions of Christians every-where. All because this man determined to daily offer praise to his God and to fill his mind with thoughts of God's glo-rious works!

⌀

I know I've said a lot about our family: Martin and me, Josie, Ben, Griffin, and Timothy. But legacies aren't just for families. You don't need to be a parent to have heirs. You don't need a spouse to leave a legacy. You and I can bless and be blessed by those who are not members of our biological families. None of us is meant to limit our focus only to those who live under the same roof with us.

I've already told you about my precious group of girl friends who are single. It's amazing to me that they've man-aged to reach this stage of adulthood without three good and wise men begging to be their husbands! They are nothing short of fantastic—all three of them. And they have poured more love and life into our family than I could begin to tell.

I met Beth, Leah, and Jackie within the first week of our move to Atlanta, fourteen years ago. To say they have become like sisters to me doesn't tell the half of it. When the twins were born and I was completely overwhelmed, Jackie began coming by our house every Tuesday night. We didn't talk about it—at least not that I remember. She didn't make a big deal about it. She just showed up and kept on showing up—ready to jump in and lend a hand (or an ear) to help us in whatever way seemed best.

She's the kind of friend that comes in and gets her own sweet tea because she knows where the glasses are. She doesn't mind changing a poopy diaper or reining in a kid that needs a firm hand. (And believe me when I say I don't mind letting her!) I don't think Jackie ever imagined singleness as a part of her story, but she's embraced it and poured her life into others in a way that humbles and inspires me. She's invested her life in our church, too, serving our lead teacher for many years as his right-hand woman. Her life is full, and she fills us up too.

The way she, Leah, and Beth have loved on our family has been something very special to all six of us. It's not unusual for the kids to wish them Happy Mother's Day, and I'm all for that. There is no way I could have done mothering without these three women in my life. I fully expect my children to rise up one day and called *them* blessed, and I'll be right behind them saying "Amen!"

You just know when you're around a surrendered life. You find yourself breathing more deeply and looking more broadly. I have another friend, Sherri, who is my mom's age. She has walked beside me through so much of my adult life, and her living example of faithfulness to God and to her family preaches to me almost every day.

It's Sherri I think of when I read Paul's instruction in Philippians to be anxious for nothing (4:6). When I struggle with anxiety or start to fret about things beyond my pay grade, her attitude of acceptance, peace, and joy helps to center me.

If you looked at her from the outside, you'd see a lovely woman from an affluent North Atlanta suburb with a caring husband, children, and grandchildren. In other words, you might see a kind of smooth and easy exterior that would lead you to imagine she doesn't have a care in the world.

I know better.

Sherri and her husband are originally from Canada and were missionaries for years in Ecuador, and I believe she thought they'd spend their lives on the foreign mission field. I don't know that Atlanta would have been her destination of choice for their later years, but when God called them, they came.

For as long as I've known Sherri, she's been mentoring other women—not as a member of our church's paid staff. Just as a friend. She and her husband, Carl, have four children. Their family is intact but is not perfect, and she doesn't pretend otherwise. Several years ago, Carl was diagnosed with Parkinson's disease, and as with most Parkinson's patients, his prognosis is not especially promising.

She could have chosen then to hunker down at home and put all her other relationships on hold. No one would have faulted her for that. It would have been easy for her to wring her hands and wonder who was coming to help *her*. Parkinson's doesn't improve with time. But Sherri demonstrates to me every day what it means to serve a husband with a disability and to do it with grace and hope and joy. I used to wonder who in the world was like that Proverbs 31 woman who actually laughs at the days ahead (Prov. 31:25). Now I know: Sherri is. I can't think of very many big decisions in my adult life that she has not been a part of. There is nothing I can't talk to her about or that I don't value her opinion on. Her wisdom has been a steady gift to me, and it's one that I mean to pass on.

I've learned from precious friends like these and others that things don't have to be a certain way for us to leave a legacy. We don't need a husband and children to pass on good things that will last. Our lives don't have to be perfect to be powerful. We can be broken and still bless others. We can be needy and still have something to give.

A woman I'll call Ann became pregnant as a teenager and was advised by the adults in her life to "fix her problem" by having an abortion, which she did. She later married and had a family, but she never told anyone about the abortion, not even her husband. So many years went by that to bring it up or speak of it seemed impossible, even though she continued to grieve her unborn child.

One Sunday Ann came to church and heard a pro-life message that cracked her heart wide open. It was as if all the grief she'd buried for years poured out at once. She went home that day and told her husband everything. His loving and tender response made her wonder why she'd waited so long to speak the truth about her past. And her surrender and honesty that day birthed something beautiful.

Ann realized that the need for postabortion healing exists not just in "the world" but in the church too. Some estimates say that one in three women in the church have experienced the trauma of abortion.

"This is my story," she decided, "but it can't be *only* my story. How many women like me are there in my church who've carried the same hurt their whole lives? And what can I do to help them heal?"

Maybe it seems strange that such a devastating experience could become an opportunity for great good, but in God's hands it has. Ann has come alongside so many women, first informally and then through a more formal ministry, who've walked the same path she has. Her legacy of sharing God's healing and forgiveness with others was born out of long years of hurting and secrecy and shame.

When we think of passing on to others the things we have of value, we don't automatically think of surrendering and sharing our heartbreak. But maybe we should. After all, our God allowed his own heart—and the body of his only Son—to be broken for you and me. And hasn't that been good?

I used to think that God would use me in a certain way or not at all. But his mercies really are new every morning, and his creativity keeps on stretching my weak imagination, day after day after day.

Writing and recording the song "Blessings" was one of the coolest things I've ever been a part of. No one could have predicted what God would do with that one song, especially not me. It would take a whole new book to tell you the connections God has made to others through those few simple words and notes; the ways he has used and keeps on using them to help and heal and speak his love are far beyond anything I ever imagined I might see.

Since then, when my record label or managers or others have suggested "Why don't you just write another 'Blessings'?" I laugh. Seriously. Very little of that song's success had anything to do with me. I wasn't out to write a hit song at all. Those were merely words from the journal of a broken woman, struggling to believe. There's nothing I did to deserve God using me to pen that song in the first place. It almost seems selfish that I would ask him to do that same thing over again!

These days I'm not asking God to use me in a particular way. I'm just asking him to use me. I may never have another monster hit like "Blessings," and that's okay with me. What wouldn't be okay would be for me to stop using the gifts he's given me. I'm not unambitious. I'm ambitious for the gospel. As long as I have breath I'll sing. And as long as he keeps on inspiring me, I'll write what I see.

My kids and my friends don't need more of my stuff. They need more of Jesus. I don't need to leave behind another "Blessings," but I have every intention of leaving behind a legacy of faith. Not mine so much, but his:

<blockquote>
I wanna give you faith
I wanna leave you hope
That you would know a love that never lets you go
More than wisdom or wealth,
</blockquote>

I Give Up

More than happiness or health,
May you say I gave you faith
Oh, and there will come a day when
you question everything
And the very ground beneath you starts to shake
And all I can offer is a prayer from far away
To the One who's never left you . . .
That he will give you faith
He'll give you hope
He'll be the love that will never let you go[1]

What legacy of surrender do you hope to leave? What will you do today to build it? No one who sets out on a journey fails to plan a route to their destination. Part of modeling surrender is being the change I want to see, right here, right now.

WHITE FLAG PRAYER #13

God, I want to be found faithful to what you've called me to. Make my surrendered life a legacy that will glorify you and help others, long after I am gone. Amen.

FOURTEEN

When I Surrender, I Worship

If you've read this far and you're still with me, thank you. We're almost done! This last chapter is one that is so very close to my heart. Anyone who knows me knows that I can't talk for long without getting around to worship. It's the thing I'm most passionate about. And worship is where we've been heading with every page of this book on surrender.

My first real job—if you don't count a few summer stints in food service—was leading worship in a local church. Perimeter Church needed a worship leader, and I was naïve enough to think that my brand-new music degree and the four guitar chords I knew might qualify me. I mean, I loved the Lord and I knew music—I could play and sing. Surely that was enough, right?

It took God no time at all to show me how unprepared I was to truly worship him, much less to help anyone else do likewise.

Four months into the job, when Martin became so ill, I struggled to stand before a congregation of people singing songs of praise to God. How in the world could I lift my voice in joy when our lives seemed to be falling apart? How could I proclaim his faithfulness when my own faith was taking such an awful pounding?

During this season of personal wrestling, my whole concept of worship began to change. I discovered that God wasn't offended if I couldn't "feel it" on a Sunday morning. Instead of worship as a warm and fuzzy, emotional experience, I began to see it as a deeper, conscious choice to praise my always-worthy God.

But getting there wasn't easy.

I began to search the Scriptures for a solid definition of worship, something I could hang my hat on when my feelings didn't automatically inspire me to praise. I didn't find a dictionary-worthy definition, but I did find plenty of people worshiping in all kinds of circumstances.

King David was most definitely feeling it when he danced his way into Jerusalem before the ark of the covenant. Removing his royal robes, David danced in the kind of simple linen garment worn by priests, celebrating with his people the visible sign of God's presence among them. (Side note: his wife was plenty upset by this; she chided him and called his display of emotion undignified, so I'm thinking it must have looked a little over-the-top.)

The book of Nehemiah records how all of Israel worshiped God together in Jerusalem on their return from exile. When the prophet Ezra read the long-forgotten words of the Law to them, including God's command to observe the

Festival of Booths, "the whole community that had returned from exile made shelters and lived in them" (Neh. 8:17 csb). And then they held a weeklong "revival":

> The Israelites had not celebrated like this from the days of Joshua son of Nun until that day. And there was tremendous joy. Ezra read out of the book of the law of God every day, from the first day to the last. The Israelites celebrated the festival for seven days, and on the eighth day there was an assembly, according to the ordinance. (Neh. 8:17–18 csb)

I even discovered Job worshiping God, not because of his situation but in spite of it. He fully acknowledged Satan's attack had left him in a real bad way:

> "For the thing that I fear comes upon me,
>   and what I dread befalls me.
> I am not at ease, nor am I quiet;
>   I have no rest, but trouble comes." (Job 3:25–
> 26 esv)

Even broken and physically afflicted, Job praised God while his life lay in shambles around him: "Naked I came from my mother's womb, and naked shall I return. The Lord gave, and the Lord has taken away; blessed be the name of the Lord" (Job 1:21 esv). Call me crazy, but I'm not picturing Job's arms raised and his eyes closed in rapture as he said these words.

These examples were helpful, and they helped me see

that worship happens in a variety of circumstances and is expressed in many different ways. But it was in the book of Romans that I finally found the answer I was looking for.

☙

The first eleven chapters of Romans contain what many theologians agree is the most comprehensive exposition of grace found anywhere in the Bible. After these eleven chapters full of rich truth, it's as if Paul took a deep breath and answered the obvious question now hanging in the air: *Considering all that Christ has done for us—making us right with God by his atoning death, freeing us from the penalty and power of sin, lavishing us with his grace—how should we respond?*

I wonder if his answer surprised them. It surprised me.

"Therefore," he wrote, "present your bodies as a living sacrifice" (Rom. 12:1 ESV). In other words, "Surrender your life, body and soul, to God. Give yourself up!"

Paul's readers would have understood the concept of sacrifice. He wrote to the first-century house churches in Rome, made up of Jewish and Roman converts to Christianity. Both groups were familiar with the practice of offering sacrifices in worship—Jewish or pagan—and both would also be reminded of Jesus' sacrifice on their behalf.

One key word in Paul's instruction showed me that he wasn't talking about a martyr's sacrifice; that word is *living*. He wasn't suggesting followers of Jesus should all die for their faith; he was asking them all to *live* for it—with lives of sacrifice that were holy and acceptable to God. This kind of surrendered life, he said, is our true and proper response. *Worship is a lived experience.*

I've heard worship described through the years in so many ways. As an hour-long service you attend on Sunday morning. As a genre of music played on your local Christian radio station. But I'd never heard it described, like Paul did, as a full-on, lifelong surrender.

When we surrender ourselves to God, we worship him. Surrendering doesn't lead us into worship; our surrender *is* our worship.

That seemed so profoundly simple!

My first response was relief. In Paul's worship paradigm, surrender outranks emotion. Of course, worship of God engages our emotions, but for Paul emotion wasn't the main requirement. Surrender was. The proper response of people who have been given everything is to present their very lives to the one who has given them everything. This is our reasonable act of worship.

My second response was a feeling of apprehension. Hold on now—a holy and blameless sacrifice? Me? Anyone who has ever met me knows I wouldn't qualify for *that*. And Paul himself already said that all of us have sinned and fallen short of God's glory. I can't present myself as a holy and blameless sacrifice on the basis of my track record. But I *can* present myself to God as holy and blameless based on his mercy!

God does not expect perfection from his children. What a relief that is! When he looks at each one of us, he doesn't see the skeletons in our closet, our self-centeredness gone rogue, our past failures, or even our potential for future failure. Before he sees anything else, he sees in us the righteousness of Jesus. We don't surrender our lives to God to gain his favor. We offer ourselves to him in response to the favor he's already freely shown us because of the saving work of Jesus!

Paul's words finally relieved me of my mistaken notion that worship is something that's done out of sheer, sustained joy in the Lord. I've heard worship referred to as "worth-ship"— literally a time to show God his worth—and the worth of God is not something that depreciates or fluctuates over time. It's solid. Constant. Steady. So even though we may go through hard seasons when our hearts fail us, worship is still a reasonable act.

No matter how I may feel about worshiping God in the moment, "The duty," said C. S. Lewis, "exists for the delight."[1] When we worship in response to God's worth, Lewis likens us to "people digging channels in a waterless land, in order that when at last the water comes, it may find them ready."[2]

Does it sound strange to be that matter-of-fact about something as powerful and potentially life changing as worship? It shouldn't. Not if your intent is to be a sacrifice. Not if your surrender is your praise.

◦ ◦

There's a beautiful story in John's gospel that illustrates for me what takes place when we worship. In the dynamic between Jesus and the Samaritan woman at the well, I see worship as God initiating, his majesty being displayed, and people responding to him.

We may think that we initiate worship by coming to church or by singing a hymn or by stilling our hearts with a quiet prayer, but it's God who initiates worship. Every time. He invites us into his presence. We never come to him unbidden.

> Now when Jesus learned that the Pharisees had heard that Jesus was making and baptizing more disciples than John (although Jesus himself did not baptize, but only his disciples), he left Judea and departed again for Galilee. And he had to pass through Samaria. So he came to a town of Samaria called Sychar, near the field that Jacob had given to his son Joseph. Jacob's well was there; so Jesus, wearied as he was from his journey, was sitting beside the well. It was about the sixth hour.
>
> A woman from Samaria came to draw water. Jesus said to her, "Give me a drink." (John 4:1–7 ESV)

You can hardly imagine the social norms Jesus shattered by approaching this woman. Jewish men were not in the habit of chatting up any woman in public. Jews would never set foot in Samaria if they could help it, and if they did, you wouldn't catch them lingering at a local watering hole. And as if these three taboos weren't daunting enough, Jesus spoke to a Samaritan woman with a very dubious reputation—one he was fully aware of before the conversation ever began.

He initiated the encounter. She did not. She would not. Somehow he spoke words that seemed to put them on equal ground for an instant: he asked her for a drink of water from the well. When he did, she immediately brought up the strangeness of his speaking to her at all: "'How is it that you, a Jew, ask for a drink from me, a woman of Samaria?' (For Jews have no dealings with Samaritans)" (v. 9 ESV).

Listen: you and I have no entrée into God's presence until he invites us in. He is always the initiator; we are always the responder. From the first moment we believe to the last breath we breathe, every time we come into his presence, we come at his invitation. We have access to him in worship because he has made himself available to us, not the other way around!

The conversation between Jesus and this woman didn't go far before she saw that she was not dealing with an ordinary man. Speaking through metaphor and also very directly, he indicated to her that he had things she did not; he knew things that she could not. "If you knew the gift of God," he told her, "you would have asked him, and he would have given you living water" (v. 10 ESV).

Then he shocked her even more by revealing what he already knew about her identity, things she would just as soon have preferred to leave safely under wraps:

> The woman said to him, "Sir, give me this water, so that I will not be thirsty or have to come here to draw water."
>
> Jesus said to her, "Go, call your husband, and come here." The woman answered him, "I have no husband." Jesus said to her, "You are right in saying, 'I have no husband'; for you have had five husbands, and the one you now have is not your husband. What you have said is true." (vv. 15–18 ESV)

When God displays his majesty—his omniscience and his omnipotence—it's normal to feel a little overwhelmed.

A little naked. We all do. You can almost feel this woman's heart racing and the gears in her mind clicking and whirring!

He knows too much! How could he? And he's offering me something that sounds impossible—but so, so good! Living water? Never being thirsty again? Who could give that? And how? And why would he, to me?

Pastor and author John Ortberg has said that when God shows up, people tend to get "blown away" and "beg for mercy."[3] Paul was struck blind by him (Acts 9:1–9). Zechariah was struck dumb (Luke 1:5–22). Isaiah cried, "Woe is me! For I am lost," and confessed he was not fit for God's presence (Isa. 6:1–5 ESV). His majesty is simply too much for us. His power is too great.

I love how writer Annie Dillard described the awesome "otherness" of God and how absurd it is that we could remain so very near but unaware of it:

> Does anyone have the foggiest idea what sort of power we so blithely invoke? Or, as I suspect, does no one believe a word of it? The churches are children playing on the floor with their chemistry sets, mixing up a batch of TNT to kill a Sunday morning. It is madness to wear ladies' straw hats and velvet hats to church; we should all be wearing crash helmets. Ushers should issue life preservers and signal flares; they should lash us to our pews.[4]

If we're not overwhelmed when God's majesty is displayed before us, I wonder if it's really God we've encountered. If we're not undone, are we really getting it?

When the Samaritan woman saw that she was fully

known by Jesus and not rejected, the real conversation began—and it centered on worship:

> The woman said to him, "Sir, I perceive that you are a prophet. Our fathers worshiped on this mountain, but you say that in Jerusalem is the place where people ought to worship." Jesus said to her, "Woman, believe me, the hour is coming when neither on this mountain nor in Jerusalem will you worship the Father. You worship what you do not know; we worship what we know, for salvation is from the Jews. But the hour is coming, and is now here, when the true worshipers will worship the Father in spirit and truth, for the Father is seeking such people to worship him. God is spirit, and those who worship him must worship in spirit and truth." (John 4:19–24 ESV)

Very soon, he was telling her that things like geography and racial history would no longer have any bearing at all on how God's people would worship him. The marks of rightly directed worship would not be external but internal. Every heart that worshiped him in spirit and truth would be the heart of a true worshiper.

Finally, Jesus revealed his identity to her in a way she could not possibly mistake or deny. She'd heard of Messiah. She had some hint of faith that he was coming, and when he came, she was confident that her questions would be answered:

> The woman said to him, "I know that Messiah is coming (he who is called Christ). When he comes, he will tell us all things." (v. 25 ESV)

Responding to that tiny expression of faith, Jesus said to her, "I who speak to you am he" (v. 26 ESV).

We can get so caught up in the trappings of our worship. In church we ask ourselves: How did the sanctuary look? Was it full? Near full? Was the soloist on key and did the strings come in on the right measure? Did the pastor's message seem to speak to me, or did it leave me indifferent or confused? Even alone we might wonder: *Did my prayer even get through to God? Did I pray long enough? Praise him enthusiastically enough?*

In all of these questions we are looking to ourselves, but not to him. We're getting closer to worship "in spirit and truth" when the externals fall away and our focus is only on him.

Finally, this story shows me that it's impossible to have an encounter with God and come away from it unchanged. Look at how the Samaritan woman responded to Jesus:

> So the woman left her water jar and went away into town and said to the people, "Come, see a man who told me all that I ever did. Can this be the Christ?" They went out of the town and were coming to him. (vv. 28–30 ESV)

This five-times-married woman who came to a well at midday to avoid the stares and whispers of her neighbors headed straight to the middle of town and said to anyone who would listen to her, "You've got to meet this man. He's extraordinary. Really. Come with me. You'll see." She didn't just leave her water jar behind at the well. She left her shame there too. She was changed, and her encounter with him was the reason why.

Worship is not something that can be learned in a class-room or perfected with the help of a textbook. It's way more hands-on than that! Worship is the lived experience of offering myself, moment by moment and day by day, to a living God. It is opening my hands and letting go of whatever I am clinging to instead of him. It is acting as if everything he says about himself and about me is absolutely true.

When I surrender my life as a sacrifice to God, I am worshiping him. Every moment of prizing God is a reordering of my own status. He reigns. Therefore, I do not. He rules. Therefore, I do not. He is sovereign. Therefore, I am not.

When I say, "Not my will, but yours, God," I am worshiping.

When I say, "I don't know what's best for me, God. But I believe that you do, and I'm going to trust you," I am worshiping.

When I say, "I like my plan, God, but if you have a better one, replace mine with yours," I am worshiping.

When I serve others before pleasing myself, I am worshiping.

When I want reconciliation more than I want to be seen as right, I am worshiping.

When I look for ways to leave my faith behind so that others can be blessed when I am gone, I am worshiping.

If the thought of opening your hands to God and offering him your life sounds too scary, too big, too terrifying, try this.

Surrender the moment in front of you right now.

Pray the prayer that's on your heart today, this moment, even if you're not sure of the words. (He's promised to help with that too!)

Help the person in need standing before you now, today.

Steal the quiet minute you have for prayer right now, instead of lamenting the half hour you don't have.

Offer God the grief that's eating at the edges of your heart today. It will only be bigger tomorrow.

Forgive the person who's hurt you today. Don't wait. Do it now.

Confess the wrong you're sick over this minute, and fall into the bottomless forgiveness of God. He's waiting. He's right here.

This is the moment for your surrender and for mine. Yes, we'll take three steps forward and two steps back some days. No matter. Take the steps anyway. Take them now.

I don't want to be in charge. Really, I don't. I just want to be his. When we surrender, we invite God into our story as our King, and we take our rightful place in his story as beloved children and heirs. That kind of surrender is the real secret to joy—joy that is never threatened by circumstances that change day to day. It leads to a life that is "adventurously expectant, greeting God with a childlike 'What's next, Papa?'" (Rom. 8:15–17 THE MESSAGE). Who wouldn't release their attempts to control life's crazy twists and turns to live like a fearless, well-loved child instead?

I give up. How about you?

WHITE FLAG PRAYER #14

God, may my moment-by-moment surrender bring you honor, glory, and praise forever! Thank you for the joy I'm finding as I raise my white flag to you with a heartfelt, "I give up."

Acknowledgments

To use the word *thanks* seems far too small a word for the debt of gratitude I owe the following people:

To Perimeter Church, this book is just a sliver of the great theology you have imparted to me. This community has been our home for fifteen years now, and you are truly family to us. A special thanks to Randy, Carol, Jackie, Bill, and Sherri for believing in me, putting up with me, and being the best parts of any book I ever write.

To Leigh, it has been a privilege to partner with you. You are one of the most gifted writers I've ever met, and I am forever one of your biggest fans!

To Nicole, my friend, coworker, and co-conspirator for all our wild adventures, thanks for many great years of working together and for talking me into writing this book!

To our family at W Publishing and HarperCollins Christian Publishers, you guys have been amazing to work with, and I appreciate you trusting me enough to partner with me again. Debbie, you are my hero! TJ, Sara, Mark,

Acknowledgments

Chad, Jon, Jay, and Amy, thanks for making me look way better and sound way smarter than I actually am. I'll make and remake a DVD with you anytime!

To Fair Trade Services, 25 Artist Agency, Stone Island Group, Compassion International, and so many other ministry partners, thanks for laying the groundwork for countless ministry opportunities for me to share this book!

Lastly, to my family: To the four grandparents who watched kiddos so I could finish manuscripts, thank you, thank you, thank you! To Martin, Josie, Ben, Griffin, and Timothy, thanks for your patience and for being willing to be talked about in this book. God has used each of you in my life to leave an indelible impression of his love and grace. Love you so much.

Notes

Epigraph

1. Laura Story, "I Give Up," © 2019 Laura's Stories and Songs (ASCAP).

Chapter 1: A Life Beyond Control

1. C. S. Lewis, *Mere Christianity* (San Francisco: Harper One, 2000), 198.
2. Laura Story featuring Mac Powell, "Open Hands," by Laura Story and Seth Mosley, track 2 on *Open Hands*, Fair Trade, 2017. Copyright © 2016 CentricSongs (SESAC) Laura Stories/New Spring Publishing (ASCAP); 2 Hour Songs/Centric Songs (SESAC). All rights reserved. Used by permission.

Chapter 3: A Great, Good, Trustworthy God

1. Sally Lloyd-Jones, *The Jesus Storybook Bible* (Grand Rapids: Zondervan, 2007), 36.
2. Laura Story, "I Can Just Be Me," by Jason Ingram and Laura Story, track 3 on *God of Every Story*, Fair Trade Services, 2013. Copyright © 2013 Laura Stories (ASCAP) New Spring Publishing Inc. (ASCAP) (adm. at

CapitolCMGPublishing.com) Sony-ATV Timber Publishing/
Open Hands Music (SESAC) So Essential Tunes (SESAC)
(adm. at EssentialMusicPublishing.com). All rights reserved.
Used by permission.

Chapter 4: A God Who Knows

1. See Matthew 1:1–17.

Chapter 5: A God Who Loves Me

1. Timothy J. Keller, *The Meaning of Marriage: Facing the
Complexities of Commitment with the Wisdom of God*
(New York: Penguin, 2013), 44.
2. Laura Story, "You Gave Your Life," by Laura Story, track 9
on *God of Every Story*, Fair Trade Services, 2013. © 2013
New Spring Publishing/Laura Stories (ASCAP). Copyright
© 2015 Laura Stories (ASCAP) New Spring Publishing Inc.
(ASCAP) (adm. at CapitolCMGPublishing.com). All rights
reserved. Used by permission.
3. C. S. Lewis, *Prince Caspian* (New York: HarperCollins,
2002), 148.

Chapter 6: A God Who Keeps His Promises

1. Laura Story, "He Will Not Let Go," by Laura Story, track
11 on *God of Every Story*, Fair Trade Services, 2013.
© 2013 New Spring Publishing/Laura Stories (ASCAP).
Copyright © 2011 Laura Stories (ASCAP) New Spring
Publishing Inc. (ASCAP) (adm. at CapitolCMGPublishing.
com). All rights reserved. Used by permission.

Chapter 7: Surrender by Letting Go

1. N. T. Wright, "Christian Origins and the Resurrection of
Jesus: The Resurrection of Jesus as a Historical Problem,"
Sewanee Theological Review 41, no. 2 (1998): 107–56.

Chapter 8: Surrender by Choosing to Believe

1. C. S. Lewis, *Letters to Malcolm, Chiefly on Prayer* (New York: HarperOne, 2017), 2.
2. Laura Story, "God of Every Story," by Laura Story and Ed Cash, track 5 on *God of Every Story*, Fair Trade Services, 2013. Copyright © 2013 New Spring Publishing/ Laura Stories (ASCAP) Alletrop Music (BMI) (adm. at CapitolCMGPublishing.com). All rights reserved. Used by permission.

Chapter 9: Surrender by Acting "As If"

1. Laura Story, "Every Word You Breathe," by Laura Story and Hank Bentley, track 8 on *Open Hands*, Fair Trade/Columbia, 2017. © 2017 Laura Stories/New Spring Publishing (ASCAP); Bentley Street Songs/All Essential Music (ASCAP). Copyright © 2017 Laura Stories (ASCAP) New Spring Publishing Inc. (ASCAP) (adm. at CapitolCMGPublishing.com). All rights reserved. Used by permission.

Chapter 11: When I Surrender, Relationships Can Heal and Thrive

1. Laura Story, "Grace Abounds," by Laura Story, track 11 on *Open Hands*, Fair Trade/Columbia, 2017. © 2017 Laura Stories/New Spring Publishing (ASCAP). Copyright © 2017 Laura Stories (ASCAP) New Spring Publishing Inc. (ASCAP) (adm. at CapitolCMGPublishing.com). All rights reserved. Used by permission.

Chapter 12: When I Surrender, Reconciliation Is Possible

1. John Piper, "Jesus Is the End of Ethnocentrism" (sermon), Bethlehem Baptist Church, January 20, 2002, https://www.desiringgod.org/messages/jesus-is-the-end-of-ethnocentrism.
2. Randy Pope, "Greater Love: One Family, Part Two"

(sermon), Perimeter Church, February 25, 2018, https://www
.perimeter.org/series/view/greater-love/.

3. See Leviticus 26 and Nehemiah 1 for examples of this.

Chapter 13: When I Surrender, I Leave a Legacy

1. Laura Story, "Give You Faith," by Laura Story and
Hank Bentley, track 4 on *Open Hands*, Fair Trade, 2017.
Copyright © 2017 Laura Stories (ASCAP) New Spring
Publishing Inc. (ASCAP); Bentley Street Songs (ASCAP)
(adm. at CapitolCMGPublishing.com). All rights reserved.
Used by permission.

Chapter 14: When I Surrender, I Worship

1. C. S. Lewis, *Reflections on the Psalms* (New York:
HarperOne, 2017), 97.

2. Lewis, 97.

3. John Ortberg, foreword to Mark Labberton's *The
Dangerous Act of Worship: Living God's Call to Justice*
(Downers Grove: Intervarsity Press, 2007).

4. Annie Dillard, *Teaching a Stone to Talk: Expeditions and
Encounters* (New York: Harper & Row, 1982), 40–41.

About the Author

Laura Story is a songwriter, worship leader, author, artist, and Bible teacher. Her songs—which have won Grammys, Billboard Music Awards, and Dove Awards—include "Blessings," "Mighty to Save," and Chris Tomlin's "Indescribable." She has authored two books encouraging many to see that despite our questions or circumstances, God is the ultimate author of our stories. Laura has a master's of theological studies and a doctorate in worship studies, and she has served as a worship leader at Perimeter Church in Atlanta since 2005. Her greatest joy is being a wife to Martin and mother to Josie, Ben, Griffin, and Timothy.

Stay connected with Laura
www.LauraStoryMusic.com
facebook.com/LauraStoryMusic
instagram.com/LauraStoryMusic

New Video Study for Your Church or Small Group

If you've enjoyed this book, now you can go deeper with the companion video Bible study!

In this five-session study, Laura Story helps you apply the principles in *I Give Up* to your life. The study guide includes video notes, group discussion questions, and personal study and reflection materials for in-between sessions.

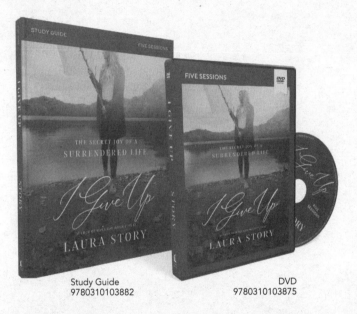

Study Guide
9780310103882

DVD
9780310103875

Available now at your favorite bookstore,
or streaming video on StudyGateway.com.

Also available: Laura's new album,
inspired by the secret of surrender.
Find it everywhere music is sold.

Is it possible that good things can come out of our broken dreams?

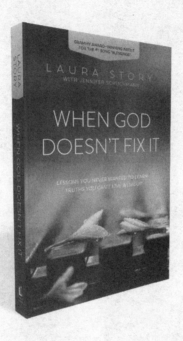

In *When God Doesn't Fix It*, Laura Story helps us understand we aren't the only ones whose lives have taken unexpected turns. She examines the brokenness of some of the heroes of our faith and shows how, despite their flaws and flawed stories, God was able to use them in extraordinary ways.

God may not fix everything. In fact, although your situation might not ever change or get better, with Jesus you can.

Check out Laura's music!

Available wherever music is sold.